John Anstie of Devizes 1743–1830

An Eighteenth-Century Wiltshire Clothier

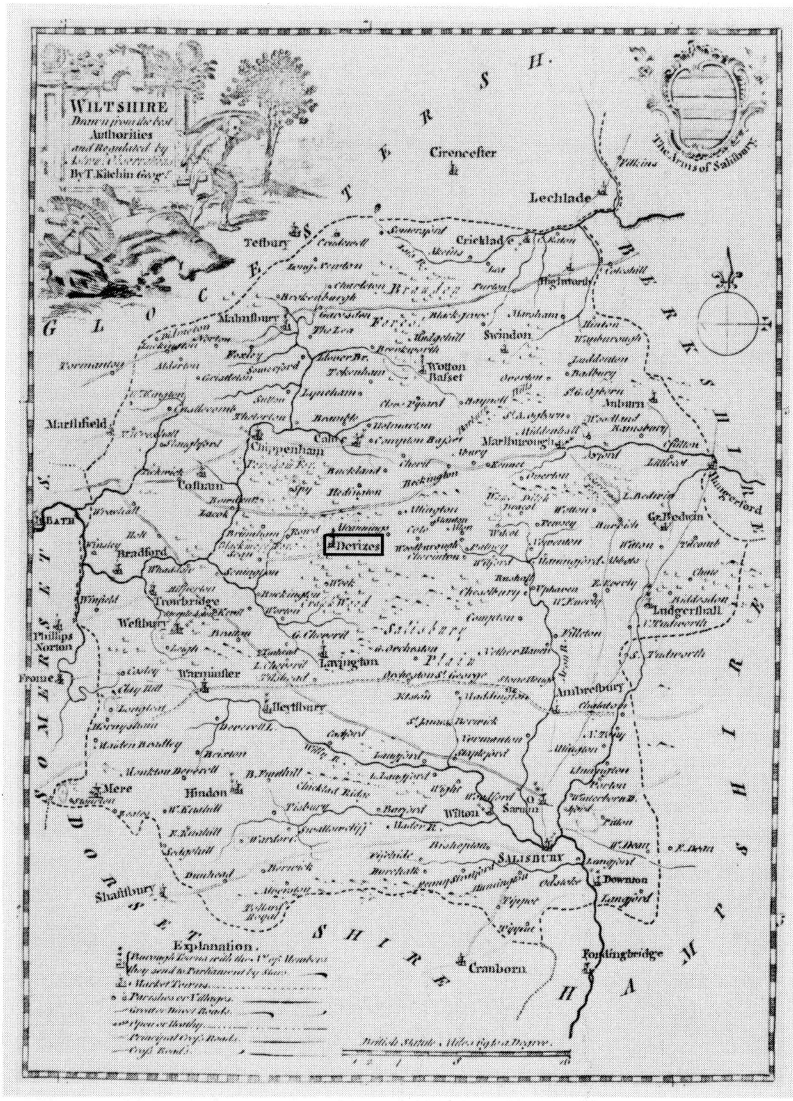

Map of Wiltshire by T. Kitchin, 1769

John Anstie of Devizes
1743–1830

An Eighteenth-Century Wiltshire Clothier

Lorna Haycock

WILTSHIRE ARCHAEOLOGICAL AND
NATURAL HISTORY SOCIETY

ALAN SUTTON

First published in the United Kingdom in 1991 by
Wiltshire Archaeological and Natural History Society
(Charity Commission No. 309534) in association with
Alan Sutton Publishing Ltd · Phoenix Mill · Far Thrupp
Stroud · Gloucestershire

British Library Cataloguing in Publication Data

Haycock, Lorna
John Anstie of Devizes.
I. Title
942.317

ISBN 0 7509 0045 8

Cover illustration: A detail from A Prospect of DEVIZES from the East *by Edward Dore (1759)*

Typeset in 11/13 Imprint.
Typesetting and origination by
Alan Sutton Publishing Limited.
Printed in Great Britain by
The Bath Press Ltd., Avon.

CONTENTS

The web of our life is of a mingled yarn, good and ill together.

All's Well That Ends Well, IV. iii. 83

Vert, a pale between two griffins segreant or

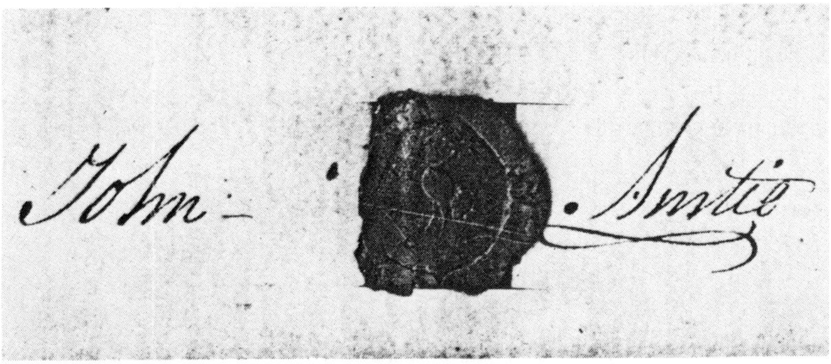

FOREWORD

By Dr Joan Thirsk

Our history of the industrial and agricultural revolutions is conventionally recounted in terms of a few heroic individuals who invented, experimented, and succeeded. We simplify things out of a necessity to explain them briefly. But such a summary overlooks much detail which would help us grasp the immensity of the changes involved. And it can induce the assumption that these revolutions were successful all along the way, when, in fact, many who tried valiantly to come to terms with their innovations experienced disappointments, near-failures, and even final disaster.

The local historian rescues us from these short-sighted generalizations by drawing attention to people of the period who shared the experience but not the enduring fame. Lorna Haycock does this admirably for John Anstie of Devizes, and so conjures up a picture of the industrial revolution from a quite fresh viewpoint. She brings to life an enterprising manufacturer of cloth in Wiltshire, who read and digested the writings of Adam Smith, and believed in free trade; in short, one who was in tune with his time. He was forward-looking, ready to experiment with new machines, new wool mixtures, and new types of cloth. He was an early builder of a factory to centralize and supervise all textile operations. But at the same time this progressive outlook was tempered by a humanity which derived from older patriarchal conventions and from a deep-seated Nonconformist faith, both of which might well have proved hindrances to business success. They were also accompanied by a pride in forming independent opinions on political controversies, preferably by gathering evidence carefully, while not necessarily running with the crowd. This attribute was likely to be a distinct asset when serving in public life. So where did this mixture of qualities take John Anstie in the late eighteenth century?

Lorna Haycock gives us a sympathetic portrait of this man, which is full of imaginative insight. She shares with us his success at first and then his failure. In the context of his time, it is a sobering story, exposing an unusual view of the industrial revolution and the price that was paid for it. The author also shows the enduring marks which John Anstie left upon his home town of Devizes. She has given to some of its buildings an historical dimension which invests them with new meaning. Thus local history accomplishes its purpose. A significant inhabitant of Devizes in the past returns to the memory of the present, as he deserves.

ACKNOWLEDGEMENTS

I should like to thank the staff of the following libraries for their help in my researches:

Bath Record Office
Bath University Library, Special Collections
The Bodleian Library, Oxford
The British Library
Devizes Library
Gloucestershire Record Office
House of Lords Library
Public Record Office, Kew
Wiltshire Local Studies Library
Wiltshire Record Office

I must particularly thank Dr Joan Thirsk, Dr James Thomas, Dr John Chandler, Dr Kate Fielden, Mr Edward Bradby, Mr Barrie Barrett and Mrs Pamela Slocombe for their much valued help and advice in preparing this book. All the photographs were taken by Derek Parker.

Donations towards publication costs of this book are gratefully acknowledged from:

The Rt. Hon. Viscount Eccles
The Marc Fitch Fund
Kennet District Council
Devizes Town Council

ABBREVIATIONS

B.C.	*Bath Chronicle*
B.H.	*Bath Herald*
B.L.	British Library
B.R.O.	Bath Record Office
B.T.	Board of Trade
c.	Cunnington cuttings collection in W.A.S. Library
G.R.O.	Gloucestershire Record Office
G.W.R.A.	Great Western Railway Archives
H.O.	Home Office
J.H.C.	*Journal of The House of Commons*
J.H.L.	*Journal of The House of Lords*
P.R.O.	Public Record Office
(SC)	Sutro microfilm copies of the Banks Papers in the Sutro Library, San Francisco
S.J.	*The Salisbury Journal*
V.C.H.	*The Victoria History of the Counties of England* (Wiltshire)
W.A.M.	*Wiltshire Archaeological and Natural History Magazine*
W.A.S.	Wiltshire Archaeological and Natural History Society
W.C.	Wiltshire Cuttings Collection in W.A.S. Library
W.R.O.	Wiltshire Record Office
W.R.S.	Wiltshire Record Society
W.T.	Wiltshire Tracts Collection in W.A.S. Library

Abbreviations

John Anstie's Pamphlets:

An Answer	*An Answer to Those who have read Sir John Dalrymple's Pamphlet in support of a Tax and Permission to export raw wool* (1782)
General View	*A General View of the Bill presented to Parliament during the last Session for preventing the illicit Exportation of British Wool and Live Sheep* (1787)
Letter to Edward Phelips	*A Letter addressed to Edward Phelips Esq. on the Advantages of manufacturing the combing wool of England which is smuggled to France* (1788)
Letter 1791	*A Letter to the Secretary of the Bath Agricultural Society on the subject of a Premium for the Improvement of British Wool* (1791)
Observations	*Observations on the Importance and Necessity of Introducing Improved Machinery into the Woollen Manufactory* (1803)

NOTE ON SPELLING

The original spelling has been retained in all quotations from documents. It should be noted that Devizes was often referred to as 'The Devizes' until the late nineteenth century.

INTRODUCTION

> The Toune of Vies standithe on a ground somewhat clyvinge and most occupied by clothiars. The beauty of it all is in one streete. The market is very celebrate.[1]

Located four hundred feet above sea level, Devizes lies in the centre of Wiltshire, on a spur of upper greensand overlooking the Avon Vale to the north-west and the Vale of Pewsey to the south – 'upon an Eminence in the midst of a fruitful Vale', according to mapmaker Edward Dore. The name Devizes, from the Latin *Ad Divisas*, refers to the position of the castle built by the Bishop of Salisbury in the eleventh century on the boundaries of three manors. The town's markets and fairs became famous for corn and wool, though John Aubrey in the seventeenth century described the market as:

> a very plentifull market of everything, but the best for fish in the county. They bring the fish from Poole hither.[2]

Celia Fiennes judged Devizes to be:

> a very neate little town with a very good market house and town hall sett on stone pillars; it is a bourrough and a very rich tradeing place for the clothing trade.[3]

The turnpiking of the roads increased the town's economic prosperity; the first local road was turnpiked in 1706 and by the mid-eighteenth century a route from London to Bath ran over the Downs by way of Devizes. Trade was centred on serge, a material popular with country folk, and drugget, a lightly woven cloth. Local clothier dynasties such as the Webbs, Suttons and Paradices emerged, occasioning Defoe to comment in 1724: 'The Devizes is full of wealthy clothiers – making mixed cloths such as are usually worn by the better sort of people.'[4] Most of the houses were then still timber-framed, being described in *The Universal British Directory* of 1791 as 'old and for the most part

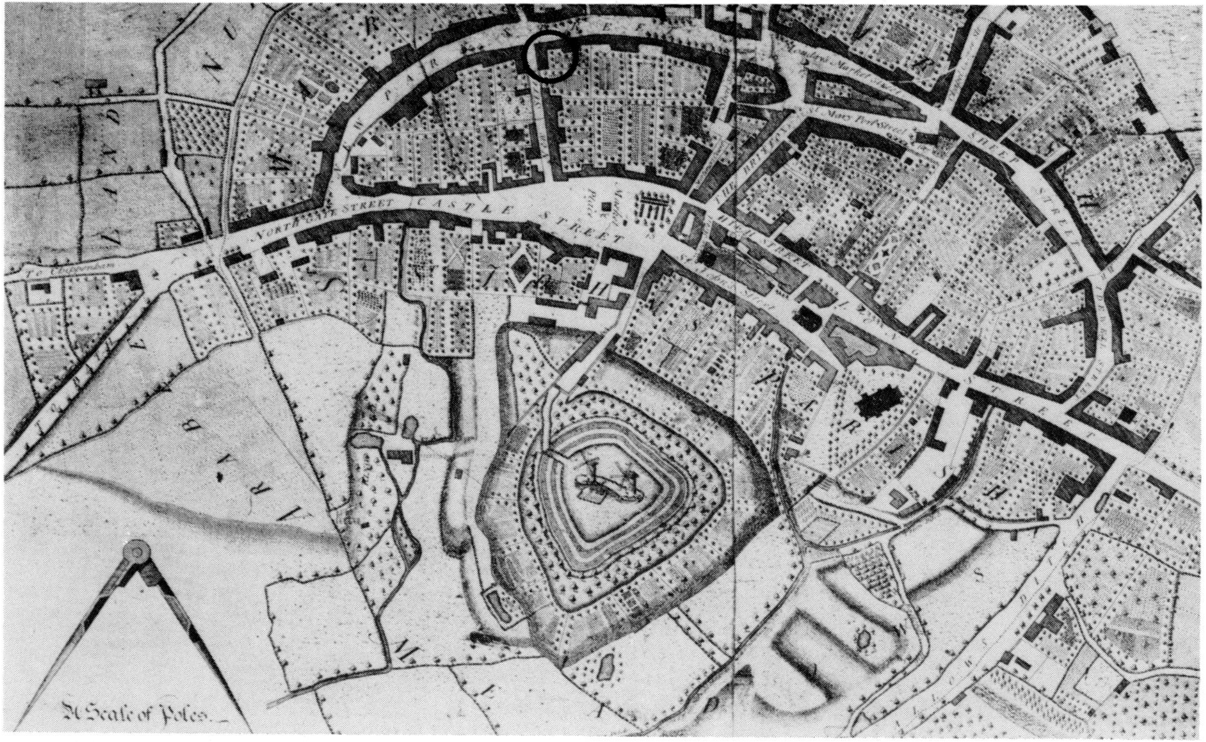

Part of Edward Dore's plan of Devizes of 1759. The site of Anstie's factory is circled

of timber, yet the model of them being good, they look tolerable'. The generation of local wealth, however, led to a spate of brick building and stone refacing in the areas of Long Street, New Park Street and the Market Place. John Britton, writing in *The Beauties of Wiltshire* in 1801, referred to the town as:

> a large and populous place, consisting of several streets which are paved. The houses are mostly built with brick, and being erected at different periods, and by various landlords, are devoid of regularity; many of them bear evident appearance of antiquity.

Edward Dore's map of 1759 (see opposite), showing the layout of the town with its belt of nursery gardens and tenter racks for drying cloth, fossilises the town's origin and its mediaeval street pattern.

On the outer periphery of this ellipse stands a four-storey rectangular factory, built by an enterprising eighteenth-century clothier, John Anstie, which he described as 'a manufactory of no inconsiderable extent'. Believing that 'there never was a greater desire manifested for Fabrics in which wool is used than at present',[5] he led the way in introducing new materials and production methods, which suggests a more enlightened and progressive attitude than the traditional view of conservative West Country clothiers. With a wage bill of £250 a week,[6] he must have been the major employer in a town of 3,000 inhabitants, but his fame and influence spread far beyond Devizes, and in economic, political, civic and religious spheres, his career draws together many threads of late eighteenth-century life.

REFERENCES

1. Leland, J., *Journey Through Wiltshire* (Henry Bull, Devizes, n.d.), p. 49.
2. Aubrey J., *Wiltshire* (Punch Bowl Press, 1984), p. 16.
3. Fiennes, C., *The Journeys of Celia Fiennes* (ed. C. Morriss, Cressett, 1949), p. 8.
4. Defoe, D., *Tour Through Great Britain* (1959), p. 280.
5. Anstie, J., *A General View of the Bill Presented to Parliament for Preventing the Illicit Exportation of British Wool and Live Sheep* (1787), pp. 22, 113.
6. W.R.O., 212A/25, Anstie Papers.

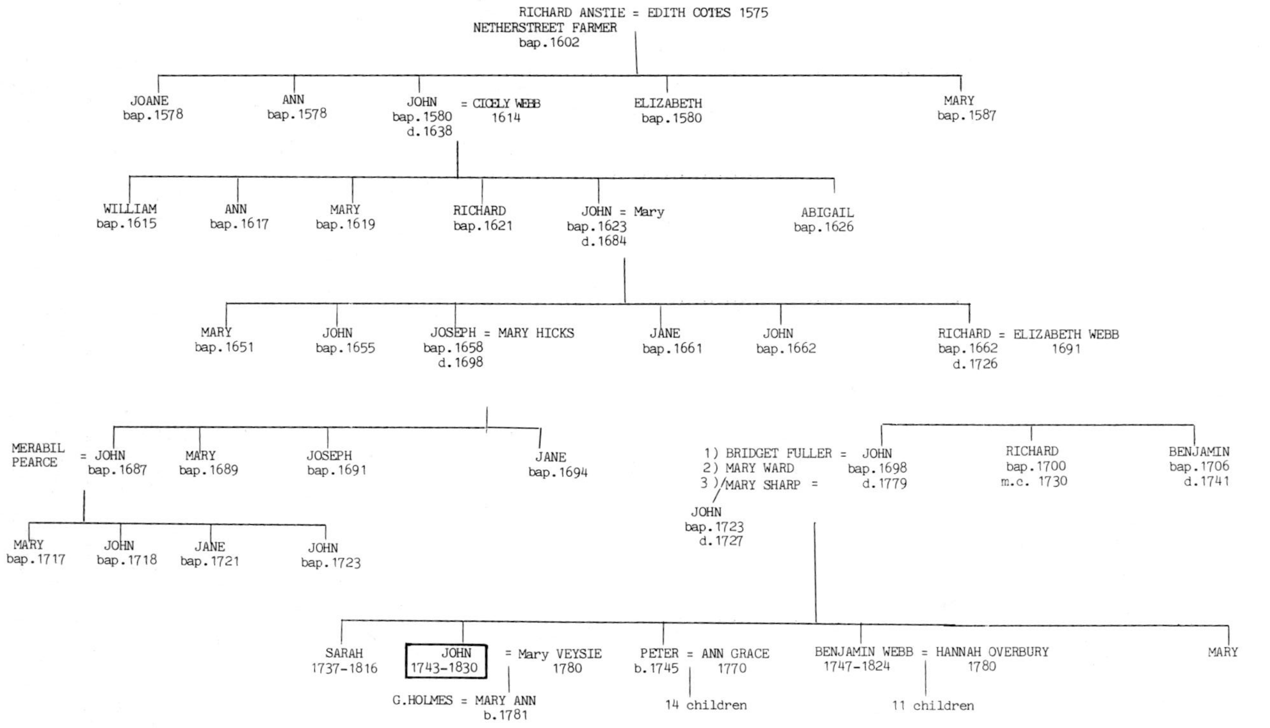

The Anstie Family Tree

CHAPTER ONE

John Anstie, the Clothier

In vain will a town, a country or a nation hope to preserve its manufactures if a lethargic torpor binds it to an adherence to old modes.

John Anstie, 1803

A prominent Devizes trading family, the Ansties originated in Battle, Sussex, and were connected by marriage with the Bayntun family of that county. Sir Edward Bayntun, Vice-Chamberlain and Vice-Chancellor to three of Henry VIII's Queens, was granted Bromham Manor after the dissolution of Battle Abbey in 1537.[1] There is a family tradition that an Anstie was at the same time Court tailor and resided at Battle Abbey after the dissolution. The Ansties probably acquired land in Bromham as a result of the Bayntun connection and they appear in the parish registers there from 1570. A late seventeenth-century descendant, Richard Anstie, Netherstreet clothier and farmer, married Elizabeth, daughter of Devizes clothier, Benjamin Webb, in 1691 and had three sons, John, born in 1698, Richard, in 1700 and Benjamin in 1706. The parish registers record his gift of 20*s*. to the poor of Bromham in 1697. Moving to Devizes a year later because of a depression in the woollen trade, he bought a grocery business on the corner of New Street and the Market Place from Mrs Lucy Hillier and was granted a ninety-nine-year lease of the premises by the Corporation.[2] Like many other clothiers, he evidently believed there was safety in diversification, selling pepper, spices and tobacco alongside his cloth, and taking advantage of the growing popularity of snuff, which he may have ground individually for each customer; a bell

Devizes Market Place in 1887. Richard Anstie's shop is in the centre of the picture

used by the Ansties for pounding tobacco bears the date 1723. Richard Anstie was a man of some substance, appearing as one of the trustees of the Elm Tree property in 1704,[3] and as a freeholder in the 1705 and 1713 Shire Poll books. His second son, Richard, was a juror at the Ruth Pierce inquest on 26 January 1753,[4] and his name is inscribed on the Punch Bowl of the Brittox Club, now in the possession of the town council. The elder Richard retained his land in Bromham, renewing a 1691 lease from Henry Bayntun of eighteen acres 'in the Cley' in 1709 at an annual rent of 6*s*. and service at Bromham Court. In

St John's Street, Devizes, with the Wool Hall, *c.* 1750

John Anstie (Sen.), 1698–1779

his will, dated 1726, the eldest son, John, was left £10,[5] and carried on the business, also acting as Sun Fire Insurance agent in Devizes.[6] He was described early in August 1751 as 'shop-keeper, snuffmaker and clothier',[7] with interests in malting and the drink trade, but he evidently became more interested in the snuff side of the business. In 1729, when he took on an apprentice, he was described as 'grocer',[8] but a *Salisbury Journal* advertisement for October 1760 announced:

John Anstie of Devizes, snuff maker and grocer, designing principally to

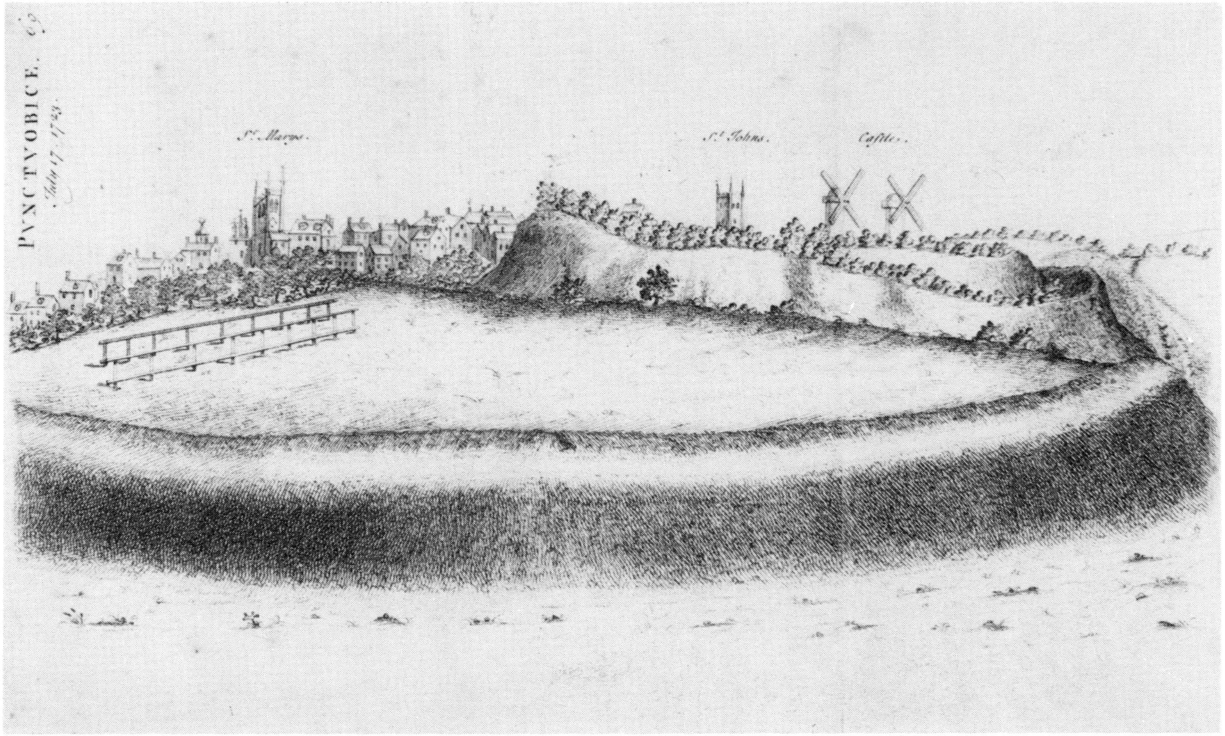

William Stukley's drawing of Devizes 1723, showing windmills on the castle site

carry on the manufacturing of snuff and tobacco, is now selling off his stock in trade, consisting of grocery and haberdashery wares, dye stuff – spirituous liquors, fine old red and white port.

On 8 December 1740 he agreed with wiremaker William Leach to become partners in the business of making and selling snuff, using two windmills on the Castle site for grinding. A year later the partnership was dissolved, Leach agreeing to erect machines for grinding snuff at Whistley Mill, held on a ninety nine year lease from the Bishop of Salisbury, and to supervise the process for one year. In return Anstie would supply him with one ton of snuff each month for his own business, the price to be regulated by the price of tobacco leaf in the Bristol market.[9]

The family bible reveals that Anstie was married three times:

Mary Anstie, née Sharpe, d. 1799

to Bridget Fuller; to Mary Ward, who died in 1731, by whom he had a son, John, born in 1723 but dying in infancy; and to the sister of a Bath surgeon, Mary Sharpe (see opposite), by whom he had six children: Peter who also died young, Sarah, John, Peter Sharpe, Benjamin Webb, and Mary. In 1776 Anstie took his sons, John and Benjamin Webb, into the business, giving each a salary of £40. The partnership lasted until the death of John (Sen.) in 1779 and his son John's decision in 1784 to specialise in the clothing business, paying £500 to quit his one-third share of the snuff trade.[10] Anstie described this change of direction in a letter of 1789:

> I was from my earliest years brought up under my father in the Tobacco and Snuff Trade – though my disposition inclined to the Clothing Business which my Father carried on in some degree after the death of an Uncle who had been considerably engaged in the Trade – My connexion with my Brother after the death of my Father continued till some four years past when my own Business becoming very intensive, I dropt all concern with the Snuff Trade.[11]

The West of England cloth trade had undergone a series of changes in the seventeenth and eighteenth centuries. Increasing competition from Dutch and German producers after the Thirty Years War hastened the decline of the white unfinished cloth export trade, and West of England clothiers had turned to production of 'the new draperies', such as medleys and drugget, introduced from France after the Restoration. In the eighteenth century the growth of the Yorkshire woollen industry, producing for the cheaper end of the market, reinforced this specialisation in superfine cloth, where there was room for expansion at home, with increasing population and wealth, and abroad in northern Europe, especially 'the new trade through Russia'.[12] Defoe remarked that Devizes had 'run pretty much into the drugget making trade',[13] and Henry Hindley of Mere wrote in 1769: 'They are making superfine cloths everywhere.'[14] Three years earlier a Bradford-on-Avon clothier, Francis Yerbury, had invented 'cassimeres', a narrow twilled cloth which could be woven extra fine but with a rib for strength, and was less heavily fulled than broadcloth. Furthermore, it could be patterned and mixed with silk, cotton or mohair for coats and waistcoats 'for the summer season at home and warmer climes abroad'.[15] The American War of 1775–83 interrupted this new trade's growth and caused hardship among the Wiltshire clothiers. A petition to Parliament presented by Burke in 1775 complained of:

> the melancholy effects therefrom – the trade of this part of the Kingdom has most sensibly declined ever since the commencement of the present and unfortunate and unnatural contest with America – chiefly owing to the merchants in Bristol not making their usual provision to furnish America – the woollen trade is very dead.[16]

With the cessation of hostilities, however, and the recent introduction of spinning machines, John Anstie saw the opportunity to exploit this new trade, which he did so successfully that he became one of the leading West Country cassimere manufacturers and a pioneer of new industrial methods.

In 1794 Thomas Davis, Steward to the Marquess of Bath, in his *General View of the Agriculture of Wiltshire* described:

> the general introduction of machines to supply the place of manual labour whereby all those parts of the manufactory that have hitherto been done in the country villages will be done at the immediate residence of the manufacturers.

The escalating use of carding, scribbling and willeying machines in cloth preparation and the complexity of the process of cassimere production led to the concentration of manufacture in large workshops. To make cassimeres, four harnesses and four treadles were required. The looms were narrow – 36 inches wide, compared with 90 inches for the normal broad loom. Their high cost and pattern intricacies made it desirable to have constant supervision of the manufacturing process, while grouping the looms in shops also prevented embezzlement of the yarn. William Stumpe had been the first to collect looms under one roof at Malmesbury Abbey in the 1540s,[17] but Government

A narrow loom for cassimeres

legislation had prevented the spread of this practice for fear of depopulation. The new coloured cloth trade, however, was outside Government regulations, and many West Country clothiers, seeing the market opportunity, began to adopt the workshop system. In 1785 John Anstie erected a purpose-built manufactory in New Park Street behind the family's grocery shop, on a site formerly occupied by a malt-house and an inn called *The Feathers*,[18] John Britton later commenting, 'Mr Anstie erected some very large premises for the purpose of carrying on the clothing trade to a considerable extent.'[19] The four storey building was of yellow stock brick, with a concealed hipped slate roof, and over one hundred windows, including bulls' eyes and large lunettes (see opposite). The interior had oak beams and elm joists, and a lead rainwater head dated 1785 bore the initials of Anstie and his wife Mary (see p. 16).[20] A *Salisbury Journal* auction advertisement in January 1794 described the building as:

> a well built clothing factory – 83 feet long, 24 feet wide – 2 wings, 18 feet by 24 feet; under the whole is a good basement storey and area, and 4 excellent stories over; also attached are shearing and weaving shops – drying house and other buildings; the land extends 140 feet in front and 190 feet deep.

There were 'lofts with receptacles for wool and yarn – a counting room' and 'various other well arranged apartments'. It was described as 'that very capacious building – The Manufactory'[21] and 'the best workshops in the County'.[22] In a street of largely two-storey timbered houses it must have been an impressive sight.

This was one of the first 'Manufactories' in the area to house the new scribbling mills and spinning jennies, described by John Britton as 'those great sources of celerity and dispatch and neatness of execution'. In 1795 Anstie's utensils in trade included:

> 20 spinning jennies, one sloobing machine, a large cloth press, 100 dozen press papers, 200 courses of handles, twisting mills, looms, willow mills, cloth racks and several hundred weight of dye stuffs.[23]

John Anstie's factory, on the right of the picture

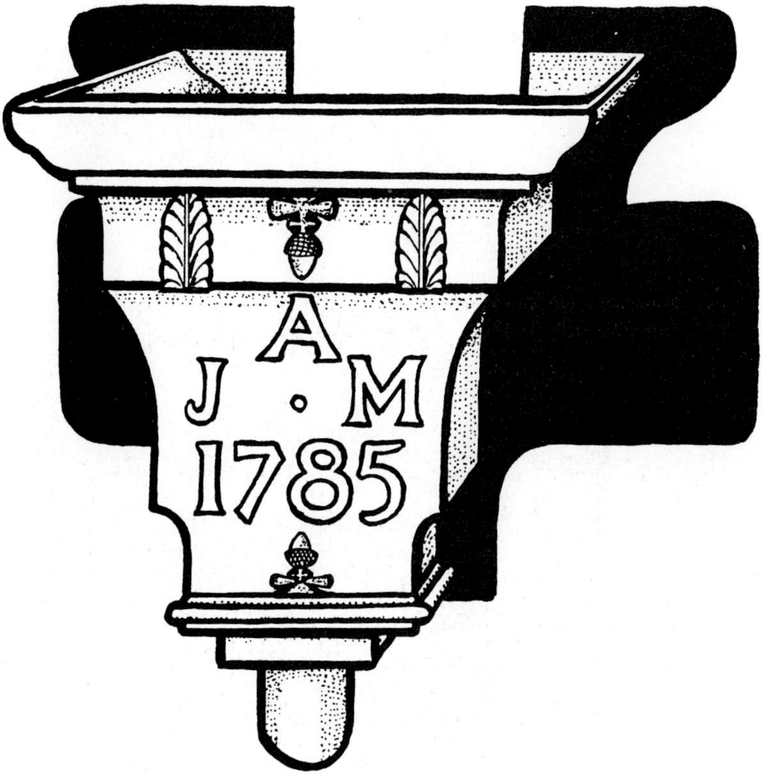

Factory rainwater head

Obviously, it was a large and complex enterprise. Contemporaries were certainly impressed, Devizes baker George Sloper noting in his diary on 10 May 1788, 'Mr John Anstie the Great Clothier keeps three hundred looms at work as he told me himself.' In many areas of Wiltshire, however, the introduction of machines was attended with considerable ferment. The new jennies and carding machines at Shepton Mallet in 1776 had led to a riot in which Warminster weavers participated, and at Trowbridge there was a disturbance when the Flying Shuttle was introduced in 1792.[24] Such was the general alarm that the bell-ringers at St. John's Church, Devizes, composed a new change:

A Spinning Jenny

Go to Trowbridge all ye weavers
Knock them down with clubs and cleavers.[25]

George Sloper noted on 14 May 1791: 'a mob at Bradford on account of the spinning and scribbling Jennies, (–) men and one woman killed of the mob. Three of them brought to the Bridewell Sunday.'

John Anstie played a leading role in trying to calm the workers' fears of unemployment and the clothiers' apprehensions of violence. Following a riot of the narrow weavers at Bradford-on-

A cloth-finishing shop. At the back a workman is raising the nap with a teasel bat. On the right are shears and shearing boards. Water was often sprinkled on the cloth to make shearing easier

Avon in February 1787, he was asked by Melksham and Chippenham clothiers to chair a meeting of the West of England cassimere manufacturers at *The George Inn*, Trowbridge, where it was agreed that weavers' and manufacturers' representatives should submit their differing views to the local J.P.s. At a further meeting on 17 February, the magistrates suggested a compromise: the manufacturers should make only fancy goods in shops while plain cassimeres could still be produced domestically. When the clothiers protested, they agreed that 'there was nothing in the practice contrary to law – and they must protect the persons and property of the manufacturers'. This did not satisfy the weavers, but they agreed 'not to be guilty of any disorder'. John Anstie confessed:

> I wish to act with the utmost impartiality. I can consider myself only in the light of an arbitrator, being very little interested in the decision of the question, as the making of plain cassimeres bears but a very small proportion to the other part of my trade.

When the Trowbridge weavers, by threat of violence, forced the manufacturers to agree to close their shops, Anstie issued a lengthy statement in the *Bath Chronicle*, refuting their assertions and adding:

> If ever there was a moment when the manufacturers ought to act in concert, it is the present one. I can safely trust to my general character as guarding me from the imputation of oppressing the poor, and I am confident that the man who with a firm temperate conduct opposes the illegal attempts of the workmen is most essentially their friend. The part which I have taken in this business is grounded simply on a determination not to submit to the menaces of a mob, and this resolution has been amply manifested in my conduct towards my own men.

Another meeting in Bath which he chaired, emphasised the inevitability of workshop manufacture, though some clothiers were still wary of erecting shops through fear of violence, and an attempt was made to calm the workers' alarm by agreeing on a minimum workshop price of 8*d*. a yard. Thanks were expressed to the chairman for 'the care he has taken to set the dispute in a just point of view, and for the sacrifice of his time and attention to the general interest'.[26]

The matter, however, continued to worry Wiltshire farmers, who, fearful of extra burdens on the Poor Rate, met in Devizes on 29 May 1794 to apply to Parliament to suppress the use of spinning machines, which 'tend much to the decrease of the Cloathing Manufactories and the injury to those employed'.[27] Later, when he had more leisure, Anstie addressed the problem in a pamphlet, *Observations on the Importance and Necessity of Introducing Improved Machinery into the Woollen Manufactory* (1803), seeking to calm 'the ferment which at present so violently agitates the minds of the workpeople in the county of Wiltshire'. (The title page is shown opposite.) He cited the cotton industry, where the introduction of machinery had led to a rapid trade increase, and referred to a conversation many years past with Sir Richard Arkwright (1732–92), who had informed him that, with proper regulation, spinners did not need to be put out of work by machines. Anstie believed that failure to adopt machinery would mean a loss of trade to Yorkshire and to countries such as France, where there was cheaper labour, and greater distress would be caused to the workpeople through loss of trade than by the introduction of machines. Technical progress, however, had to be 'combined with a just regard for the interest of the common people'. Corruption of the factory workers' morals could be avoided by 'temperate discipline, attention to decency, proper inspection and judicious modes of management'. He suggested circumspection in the introduction of machines and Government interference 'as far as it may be found consistent with the freedom of trade to guard against the evils arising from sudden alterations'. Anstie emphasised that he could never approve of anything likely to injure the workpeople; 'on the contrary he may safely appeal to the testimony of those he has employed that he ever wished to see them comfortable'. He was clearly a firm but enlightened employer, who paid fair wages and cared for his workers' welfare. In 1786 one of his clerks,

OBSERVATIONS

ON THE

IMPORTANCE AND NECESSITY OF INTRODUCING

IMPROVED MACHINERY

INTO THE

Woollen Manufactory;

More particularly as it respects the Interests

OF THE

COUNTIES OF WILTS, GLOUCESTER, AND SOMERSET;

WITH

General Remarks on the present Application to Parliament.

BY THE MANUFACTURERS,

For the Repeal of several of the existing Laws.

IN

A LETTER,

Addressed to

The Right Honourable Lord Henry Pettey.

BY JOHN ANSTIE,

Chairman to the General Wool Meeting in the Year 1788.

LONDON:

Printed by C. Stower, Charles Street, Hatton Garden, for the Author,

AND

SOLD BY STOCKDALE, PICCADILLY; VIDLER, 349, STRAND; [redacted], WHITEHALL; AND RICHARDSON, ROYAL-EXCHANGE.

1803.

Title page of John Anstie's 1803 pamphlet

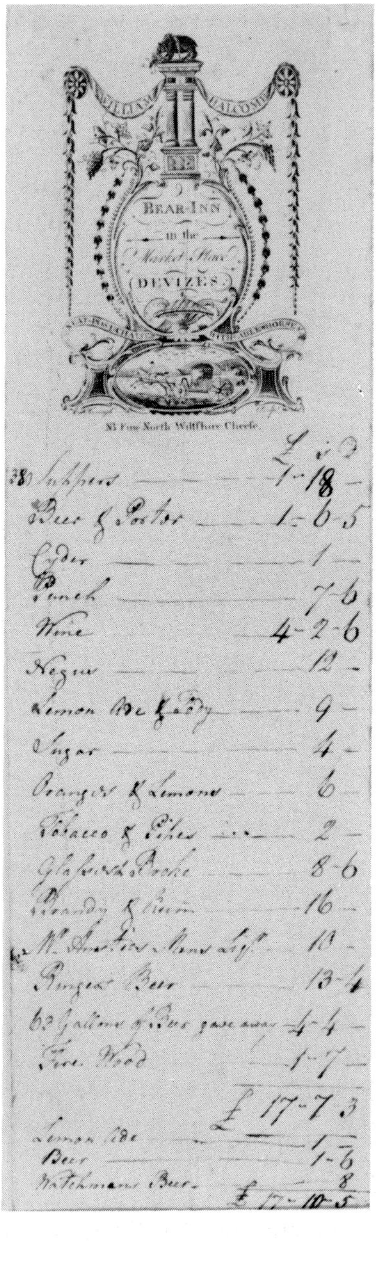
BEAR-INN in the Market Place DEVIZES

NB Fine North Wiltshire Cheese.

	£	s	d
38 Suppers	7	18	–
Beer & Porter	1	6	5
Cyder		1	–
Punch		7	6
Wine	4	2	6
Negus		12	–
Lemon Ade & Toddy		9	–
Sugar		4	–
Oranges & Lemons		6	–
Tobacco & Pipes		2	–
Glasses & Bottle Broke		8	6
Brandy & Rum		16	–
Mr. Anstie's Mens Lig.r		13	–
Ringers Beer		13	4
6½ Gallons of Beer gave away		4	4
Fire Wood		1	7
	£ 17	7	3
Lemon Ade		1	–
Beer		1	6
Watchmans Beer			8
	£ 17	10	5

A bill in the Lawrence Room of *The Bear Hotel*

Richard Cale, received £30 a year, with an annual bonus of £5, while outriders like John Collins were paid about 4*d*. an hour, with expenses.[28] Provision for his employees' comfort is illustrated in a bill in *The Bear* tabulating liquor for Mr Anstie's men. In 1808, in the midst of his own problems, he interceded on behalf of the son of a 'man who formerly with his whole family worked for me in Devizes'. Anstie wrote to Lord Hawkesbury:

> The young man had married into a bad family, but there is no probability of his again living with his wife, and, should he find mercy, I hope he may again be a good member of society.[29]

This episode illustrates considerable loyalty on Anstie's part, and also suggests that women and children were employed at his factory.

In addition to contented employees and the latest technology, high quality raw materials were important to Anstie's business. He was always especially discriminating about the quality of the wool used in his manufacture, and was prepared to experiment to offset shortages of foreign wool. At the Annual Meeting of the Bath and West Agricultural Society on 11 December 1791, it was noted that:

> he is now manufacturing a quantity of the wool of South Down sheep, which have been fed upwards of two years on the Wiltshire Downs, and that from its fineness and peculiar quality he is strongly of opinion that race of sheep may be so much improved by crossing, especially with Spanish rams, as to possess nearly the properties and value of Spanish wool.[30]

Cassimeres were made entirely of Spanish wool, but English wool was used for coarser cloth such as serges and beavers.[31] In 1794 Anstie's wool stock comprised fourteen bags of Spanish wool, twenty-one bags of Spanish lambs' wool and eleven packs of English wool.[32] Since one bag of Spanish wool would supply four pieces of cloth twenty-five yards in length and seven quarters wide,[33] this indicates a considerable production capacity. Anstie bought much of his supplies locally from the

Stephen Hillman's house in Devizes High Street.

wool merchant Stephen Hillman, whose ledgers show that in the year 1770–1 he purchased £91 worth of Sussex and Hereford wool, paying extra to have the wool pre-scoured. Between September and November 1783 he paid £145 7*s*. 0*d*., and over the period December to July 1785 he spent £205 on wool.[34] Bristol and Salisbury markets and Romsey wool auctions were other likely supply sources. He may have obtained his Spanish wool from the Spanish Consortium in London, as Wiltshire clothiers were increasingly doing in the eighteenth century. The origin of his silk is more obscure. *The Universal British Directory* of 1791 makes no mention of silk-throwing in the area; it is possible that Anstie was supplied by Willmotts of Sherborne.

A comparison of Anstie's Sun Fire Insurance policies over the years 1778 to 1786 illustrates the acceleration and centralisation of his operations. In 1778 his utensils and stock, which were stored at Edward Jeffries & Co., Blackwell Hall factors in London, amounted to £2,000. A year later he had stock worth £400 in the plaster-and-tiled premises of John Philips, and stock in the premises adjoining Seend Head Mill of £200. In 1780 two timber-and-tiled workshops adjoining his house in New Park Street, which he had bought on his recent marriage, were each insured for £300, with a total stock of £1,100. A dyehouse, Snakemead Mill, in Bishops Cannings parish was insured for £40. Stock in various rented backshops and workshops in Devizes amounted to £450, while stock at Rowde and Seend Head mills totalled £350. In 1786, his workshops, now more centralised, were insured for £600, and his utensils and stock in Devizes were valued at £800.[35] It is clear that after his father's death in 1779, when he acquired £1,386 16*s*. 10*d*. from the estate,[36] Anstie considerably expanded the clothing side of the family firm, and by 1781 was no longer using the storage facilities of Blackwell Hall, though the dispersal of his stock in rented workshops may have reinforced his inclination to centralise his operations under one roof.

Some diffusion of activity was still necessary, however, because of the shortage of water in Devizes. Although Anstie

Poulshot Mill (from an old photograph)

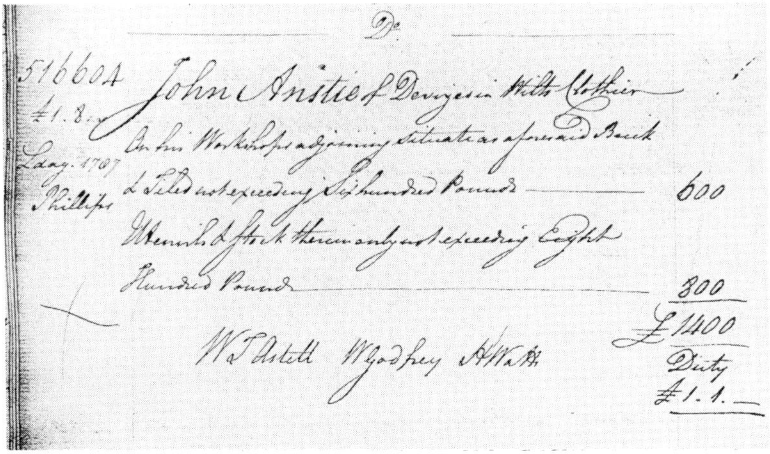

516604 John Anstie of Devizes in Wilts Clothier
£1.8.
On his Workshops adjoining situate as aforesaid Brick
& Tiled not exceeding Six hundred Pounds — 600
Utensils & Stock therein only not exceeding Eight
Hundred Pounds — 800
£1400
Duty
£1.1.

John Anstie's fire insurance policy, 1786

may have used horse power for his carding machinery at the Devizes factory,[37] he used water power for carding and spinning at Poulshot Mill, which he bought in 1791[38] and which was described three years later as 'a newly built mill with machinery for carding and spinning wool, with a large head of water'.[39] In 1777 he rented Rowde Mill from the Norris family of Bromham, acquiring the leasehold in 1788 for £750.[40] The dyehouse at Snakemead Mill, which he had purchased in 1778, had:

> seven furnaces, together with a building consisting of a fire stove, rack stove, and air stove, with a small dwelling house lately erected for the residence of a foreman – within two minutes walk from the Market Place, lately in the occupation of Mr John Anstie who fitted up the same at great expense in a very superior manner. The dyehouse is constantly and regularly supplied with water from four ponds – a nineteen foot fall may be had from the pond head.[41]

Before the cutting of the Kennet and Avon Canal, the cloth was conveyed by horse and cart through Couch Lane and along the road to the dyehouse across what is now the Canal Wharf.

Road improvements in the eighteenth century were making

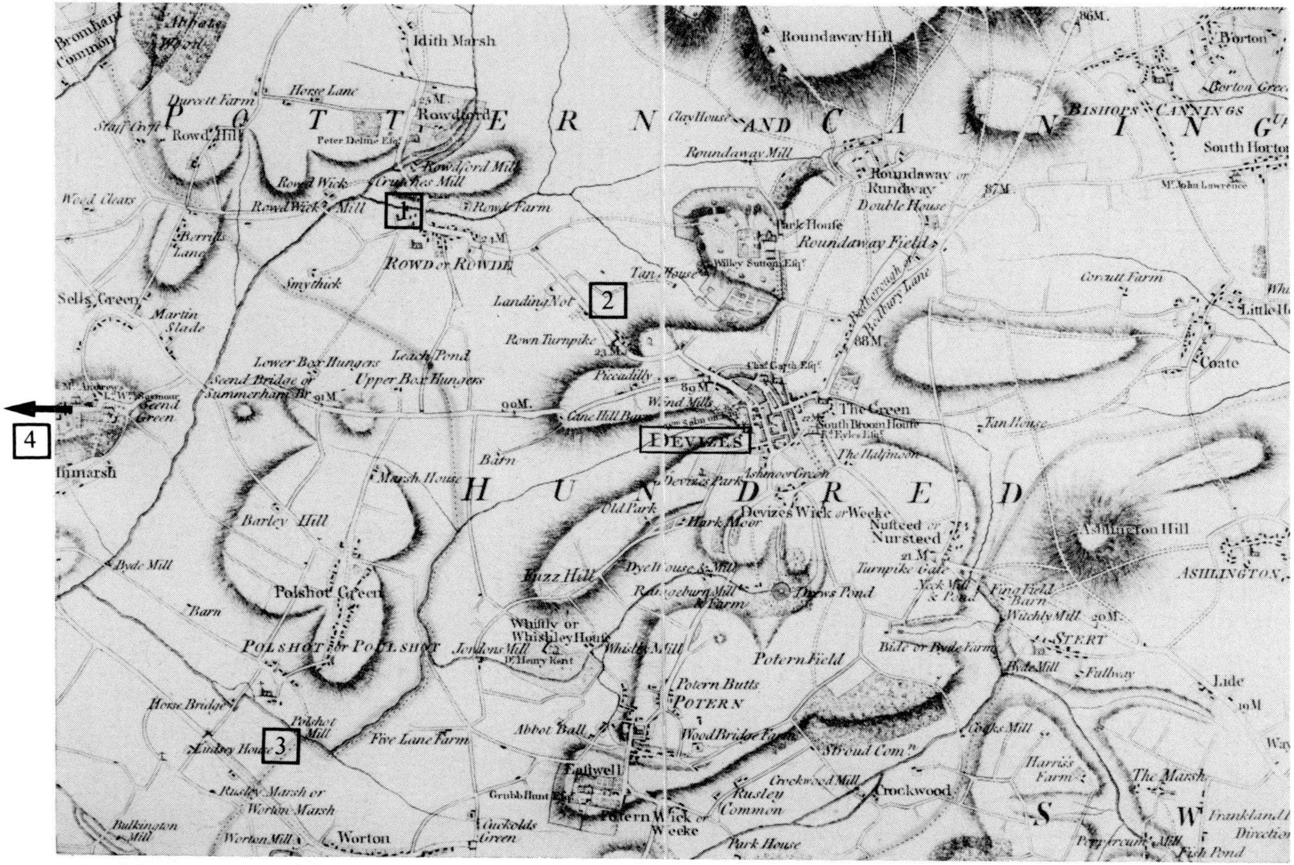

A detail from a map of Wiltshire by Andrews and Dury (1773). The location of Anstie's mills is marked as follows: 1 Rowde Mill; 2 Snakemead Mill; 3 Poulshot Mill; 4 Seend Head Mill ($1\frac{3}{4}$ miles to the west)

Seend Head Mill

Rowde Mill

Remains of Rowde Mill water-wheel

Remains of Rowde Mill dyehouse

direct contact with customers more feasible. Though not as big as Trowbridge, Melksham, Bradford or Westbury, Devizes was the site of the County Court, with an important corn market, making it an ideal business centre. Every day five stagecoaches passed through the town and there was a daily postal service to Bristol and London. Two wagons departed for Salisbury every week, and three for Bristol, Bath and London;[42] 'their general ladings were Spanish and Saxon wool down and cloth back'.[43] The Anstie account books record employees' trips to London and Romsey and ten day journeys. John Anstie was also involved in international trade, with cloth on commission in the hands of agents in Paris, Hamburg, Frankfurt, Limoges and Lisbon in 1793.[44] Even before the Commercial Treaty of 1786 with France, his goods were finding their way illicitly into Paris via Ostend, handled by a London agent, and he described this as 'an increasing trade' because of 'the avidity with which the French purchase our fancy goods'.[45] He believed that his fabrics had 'operated considerably in fixing the Taste for English woollen goods in France'.[46] An Anstie stock book of 1793, now lost, revealed that nine different kinds of mixtures were being made of wool mixed with silk – in stripes, checks, spotted and figured cloth, and altogether thirty-one distinct types or qualities of cassimeres were being manufactured. The silk striped cloth sold particularly well in Russia.[47] A few weeks before the outbreak of the French Revolution, Queen Marie Antoinette chose one of his silk cloth patterns (no. 37059) and this was forwarded to France at the end of June, together with patterns of Vicunian wool from South American sheep, dyed in rich browns.[48]

Through his political and economic activities, to be described in the next chapter, Anstie had made valuable London social contacts. The Chief Clerk to the Board of Trade, George Chalmers, was the intermediary through whom he came to supply a leading politician, Lord Hawkesbury, with cloth similar to that chosen by the French Queen. He took great trouble over this order, being vexed to find that it had been wrongly pressed; five yards were cut off and the glossiness removed before he was

St John's Street, Devizes, in the late eighteenth century (undated lithograph)

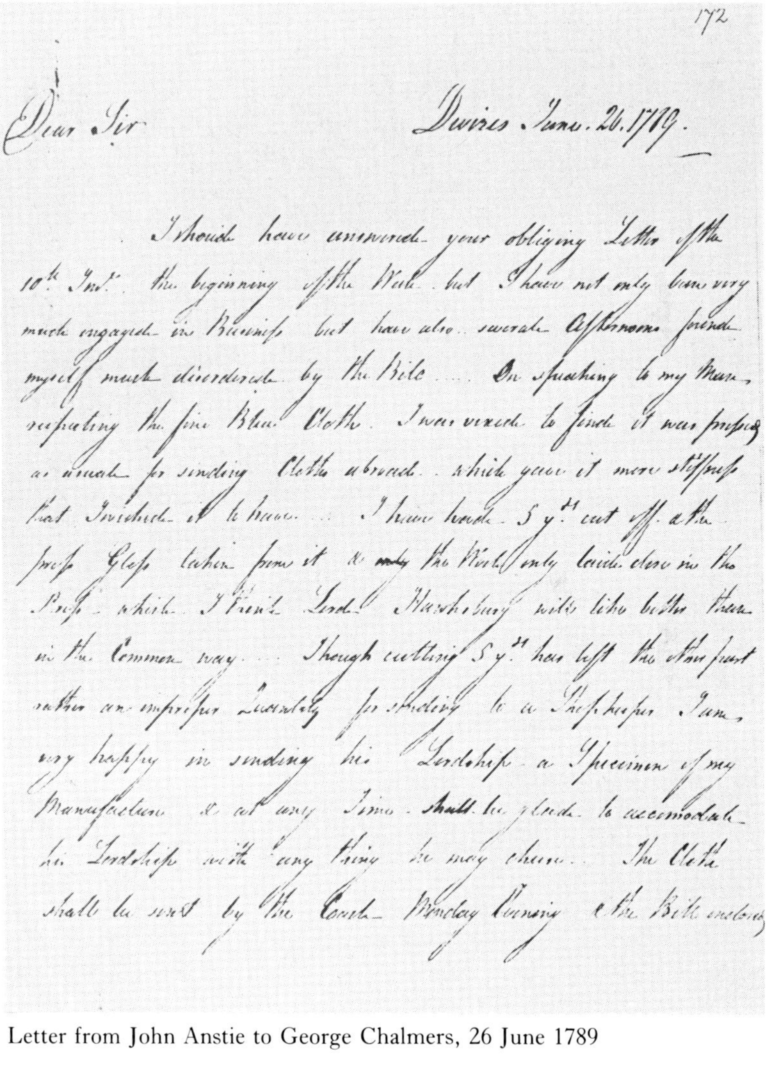

172

Dear Sir

Devizes June 26. 1789.

I should have answered your obliging Letter of the 10th Inst. the beginning of the Week but I have not only been very much engaged in Business but have also several Afternoons found myself much disordered by the Bile .... On speaking to my Man respecting the fine Blue Cloth I was vexed to find it was pressed as usual for sending Cloths abroad which gave it more stiffness that I wished it to have ... I have had 5 yds cut off & the press Glass taken from it & ~~only~~ the Work only laid close in the Press which I think Lord Hawkesbury will like better than in the Common way ... Though cutting 5 yds has left the Remnant rather an improper Quantity for sending to a Shopkeeper I am very happy in sending his Lordship a Specimen of my Manufacture & at any Time shall be glad to accommodate his Lordship with any thing he may chuse ... The Cloth shall be sent by the Coach Monday Evening & the Bill enclosed

Letter from John Anstie to George Chalmers, 26 June 1789

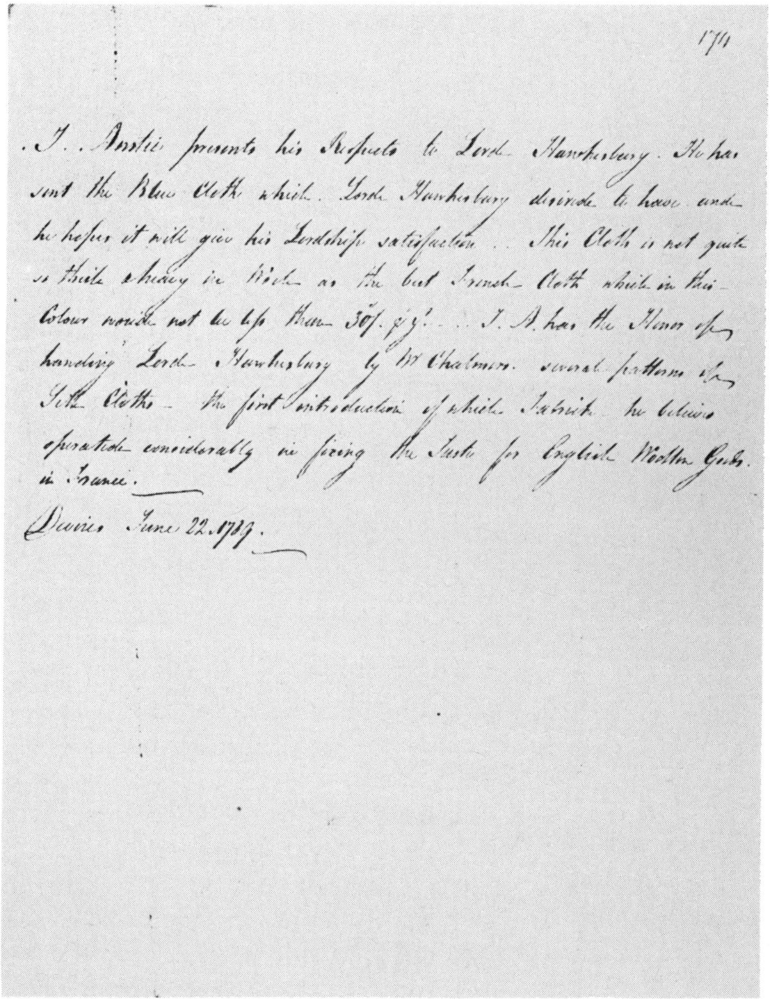
174

J. Anstie presents his Respects to Lord Hawkesbury. He has sent the Blue Cloth which Lord Hawkesbury desired to have and he hopes it will give his Lordship satisfaction. This Cloth is not quite so thick & heavy in Wool as the best French Cloth which in this Colour would not be less than 30/. p yd. ... J. A. has the Honor of handing Lord Hawkesbury by Mr Chalmers several patterns of Silk Cloths – the first introduction of which Article he believes operated considerably in fixing the Taste for English Woollen Goods in France.

Devizes June 22. 1789.

Letter from John Anstie to Lord Hawkesbury, 22 June 1789

Examples of late eighteenth-century costume.

satisfied enough to dispatch the order to London by the evening coach, with the bill enclosed. He felt that his price of 18*s*. a yard for a three-quarter yard width compared favourably with London prices of at least a guinea and a half. Lord Hawkesbury, who had great influence at Court, had promised to show some of his patterns to 'some ladies of High Rank and perhaps to the Queen'. Anstie prepared the samples meticulously and sent them by post to Mr Cothele to reach Queen Charlotte before she travelled to Weymouth.[49] She was evidently impressed and had placed an order by August, asking for other samples to be sent. Lord Hawkesbury's own order for four silk cloths was dispatched in December, together with some more patterns for the Queen, which he could not send to France, because of the 'adverse state of public affairs there'. He also sent Lord Hawkesbury a coat made of Vicunian wool, and offered to make a similar one for King George, dyed a rich purple 'should His Majesty be inclined to wear it'. He concluded: 'I must confess it will give me great pleasure to be known by His Majesty to be the principal

Manufacturer of Fancy Cloth.'[50] Anstie's national reputation as a leading manufacturer was already assured, however, by his activities in other spheres.

REFERENCES

1. *Letters and Papers, Foreign and Domestic, Henry VIII*, vol. 12, part 1, 1537, 311, 33.
2. W.A.S., Mss Box 136.
3. W.A.S., Edward Kite Mss, Pedigrees II, p. 214.
4. W.A.S., c/1/51. Ruth Pierce dropped down dead in the Market Place, 1753 'with a lie in her mouth' after declaring she had paid her share in a wheat transaction in the market.
5. W.R.O., 212A/25, Anstie Papers.
6. W.A.S., W.C., 2, p. 126.
7. Guildhall Library Mss, Sun Fire Insurance Policy Register, vol. 93, dated 5 Aug. 1751.
8. Dale, C. (ed.), *Wiltshire Apprentices and their Masters 1710–60*, (W.R.S. vol. 17, Devizes 1961), p. 167.
9. *Wiltshire Notes and Queries* (8 vols. Devizes 1896–1916), vol. 2, p. 538.
10. W.R.O., 212A/25, Anstie Account Books, 1776–1824.
11. Letter of John Anstie to Lord Hawkesbury, 16 July 1789, B.L. Add. Mss 38224.218.
12. Letter from H. Laybourne, 23 Nov. 1743, *The Gentleman's Magazine* vol. 13 (1743), p. 584.
13. Defoe, *Tour Through Great Britain*, p. 281.
14. Letter of Henry Hindley to Messrs Thomas, Williams & Co, 2 Dec. 1769: W.R.O. 372/1, Henry Hindley's Letters, 1762–70.
15. B.C., vol. XII, 589, 30 Jan. 1772, Patent 858.
16. W.A.S., W.C., 3, p. 13; *S.J.*, 1775.
17. For William Stumpe, see *V.C.H.* vol. 4, pp. 146–7.
18. Browne, W., 'Long's Stores', *W.A.M.* 55 (1954), pp. 139–45.
19. Britton, J., *The Beauties of Wiltshire* (3 vols., 1801) II, p. 308.
20. *List of Buildings of Special Architectural or Historic Interest*, Borough of Devizes, (D.o.E. 1972), p. 93.
21. *B.H.*, vol. IV, 150, 10 Jan. 1795.
22. W.A.S., W.T. 149, *Devizes in 1788, Recollections of Frederick George Hayes*.
23. *B.H.*, 10 Jan. 1795.
24. *B.C.*, vol. XVI, 822, 18 July 1776; *S.J.*, vol. LVII, 2829, 27 Aug. 1792.
25. *Devizes in 1788*; see note 22.

26. *B.C.*, vol. XXVI, 1369, 1371, 1372, 1375, 8 and 22 Feb., 1 and 22 March 1787.
27. *S.J.*, vol. LIX, 2919, 19 May 1794.
28. W.R.O., 212A/25.
29. Letter of John Anstie to Lord Hawkesbury, 4 Feb. 1808, P.R.O., H.O. 42/95. 65.
30. *S.J.*, vol. LVI, 2794, 26 Dec. 1791.
31. P.R.O., B.T. 6/106, Evidence before Committee of Privy Council.
32. *S.J.*, vol. LIX, 2915, 21 April 1794. One bag of wool weighed 200 lbs.
33. P.R.O., B.T. 6/113, Evidence of Thomas Everitt for French Treaty.
34. W.R.O., 1090/52, Stephen Hillman's Ledgers 1769–1812.
35. Guildhall Library, Sun Fire Insurance Policies (Ms 11, 936/270, 277, 287, 337).
36. W.R.O. 212A/25.
37. Rogers, K., *Warp and Weft* (Buckingham, 1986), p. 73. Joseph Phelps used a horse mill at his Bradford-on-Avon workshops in 1794.
38. W.R.O., 212B 529/230, Poulshot Mill Leases.
39. *S.J.*, vol. LIX, 2908, 3 March 1794.
40. W.R.O., 248/78, Rowde Mill Leases.
41. *S.J.* vol. LV, 3038, 5 Sept. 1796.
42. *Universal British Directory of Trade, Manufactures and Commerce* (5 vols., 1791), vol. 2, p. 778.
43. W.A.S., W.C., 5, p. 152.
44. Institute of Historical Research, Boddington Mss, Notes for *V.C.H.* (1908).
45. P.R.O., B.T., 6/113 and 114, John Anstie's evidence for French Treaty.
46. Letter of Anstie to Lord Hawkesbury, 22 June 1789, B.L. Add. Mss 38224.174.
47. Boddington Mss, loc. cit.
48. B.L. Add. Mss 38224.174.
49. Letter of Anstie to George Chalmers, 26 June 1789, B.L. Add. Mss 38224.172.
50. Letters of Anstie to Lord Hawkesbury, 7 Aug. and 7 Dec. 1789, B.L. Add. Mss 38224.248 and 349.

CHAPTER TWO

John Anstie, the National Figure

> It is the inherent birthright of an Englishman in all national questions to think and to speak for himself, if he be so inclined.
>
> John Anstie, 1782

During the 1780s John Anstie became a national political figure largely through the wool export controversy. The trade depression and the halving of long combing wool prices at the end of the American war led to the formation of the Lincolnshire Wool Growers Committee in 1782 to press for relaxation of the 1662 laws prohibiting wool exportation; wool in Europe was now fetching three or four times the price in England. Sir Joseph Banks, the scientist, and Arthur Young, the agricultural writer, became their chief spokesmen. The Leeds manufacturers retaliated, claiming that such a move would injure the kingdom's trade and manufactures and met at *The King's Arms Tavern* in Old Palace Yard, Westminster, on 28 January 1782.[1] So began a six-year struggle and bitter pamphlet warfare in which Anstie played a leading role. In 1782 he wrote a pamphlet in answer to Sir John Dalrymple's proposal to allow wool export on payment of a tax (see title page opposite). He regarded it as 'the scheme of a few disappointed monopolisers', which would 'absolutely ruin the Clothing Trade – the only staple commodity this Country has left'. The decrease in Lincolnshire wool prices he attributed to factors such as trade loss through war, the trebling in money values and the increase in wool on the market through enclosures and agrarian improvements.[2]

On 2 September 1784 Somerset woollen manufacturers called

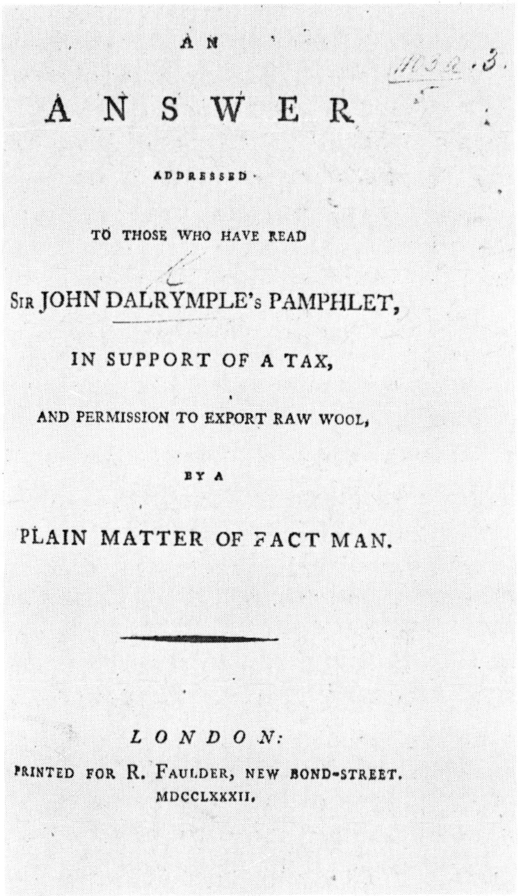
AN

ANSWER

ADDRESSED

TO THOSE WHO HAVE READ

SIR JOHN DALRYMPLE'S PAMPHLET,

IN SUPPORT OF A TAX,

AND PERMISSION TO EXPORT RAW WOOL,

BY A

PLAIN MATTER OF FACT MAN.

LONDON:

PRINTED FOR R. FAULDER, NEW BOND-STREET.

MDCCLXXXII.

Title page of John Anstie's pamphlet of 1782

a 'very numerous and respectable meeting'[3] at *The Pelican Inn*, Bristol, to protest that, through a marked increase in smuggling, there had in fact been 'an alarming decrease in wool for the manufactories'.[4] Anstie attended 'without the most distant idea of taking an active part in the business', but when he was unanimously elected to the chair, he felt that he 'could not with propriety decline'.[5] A similar meeting was held in Leeds; its resolutions were sent to Anstie and a mutual correspondence established. He chaired a subsequent meeting of delegates from eighteen counties as well as some M.P.s at *The Crown and Anchor* in the Strand on several days in December 1784. Rewards were offered for information on smuggling and a memorial was submitted to the Government, asking for stricter enforcement of the existing laws prohibiting wool export.[6] Despite assurances of ministerial support, the Irish propositions monopolised Parliament's attention, and Anstie occupied himself in 'strict investigation of the subject', drawing up plans for revised regulations, which he sent to George Rose at the Exchequer and to the Leeds Committee.[7] By 1786, however, the manufacturers had decided that nothing less than the repeal of existing laws was required, and Anstie was elected chairman of the General Meeting of Wool Manufacturers to press for a new, more effective bill.[8]

At the outset, he reminded the manufacturers that he would act 'according to the sentiments of my own mind' and that, 'should the cause in which we were engaged appear, on a fair enquiry, not capable of being supported on the ground of national benefit, I should consider myself at liberty to quit my station'. His own interests were not involved, as he used Spanish wool and English short wool, and he approached the subject with his usual impartiality, briefing himself carefully by reading Mr Smith's *Memoirs of Wool*, as 'the subject was novel to me' and almost being persuaded by the arguments in favour of wool export. He set out, however, to establish whether smuggling was carried on to any considerable extent and whether the present laws were adequate. He described his strategy:

> The liberal subscription which was entered into immediately on the formation of the General Meeting in London has enabled me to employ persons capable of procuring intelligence, and I have spared no pains or expense in order to furnish myself with such materials as, from their solidity, I doubt not are capable of combating all opposition to this proposition – that British wool is smuggled in great quantities.[9]

The information he received exceeded his most 'sanguine expectations': 'every step I advance in this enquiry leads to more important discoveries', findings which would refute the claim that the manufacturers were raising 'a clamour about a thing . . . which is of trifling consequence'.[10]

Anstie's first bill aimed to extend the regulations on shearing registration binding Kent and Sussex to the whole kingdom and to tighten up their execution. He had abstracts of existing laws distributed throughout the country, and wrote two pamphlets on the subject,[11] 'to exercise an attention to the point in dispute in men of liberal and impartial minds'.[12] Convinced of the need to prevent the French underselling the market, yet sensible of the difficulty of reconciling wool growers' and manufacturers' interests, he aimed to be 'attentive to everything that respects the general cause', and to achieve a bill 'drawn up without partiality or prejudice'.[13] Rancour, however, soon appeared in the publicity of both sides. A farming M.P., Lord Sheffield, accused the bill's sponsors of wanting to restrict the conveyance of wool to the Northern manufacturers out of jealousy,[14] and Pemberton Milnes, a Lincolnshire landowner and Yorkshire wool merchant, also believed that the real motive in the West Country was to

> stab our Yorkshire and Lancashire trade to the heart by depriving us coming at the raw materials – the bill ought to be burnt at the Market Cross in every Town in the Kingdom.[15]

Arthur Young considered the bill 'a conspiracy of the manufacturers against the landed interest', binding the wool growers in 'shackles of iron'.[16] For this reason Anstie shrewdly addressed one of his pamphlets, the *General View*, to an acquaintance, one of the leading Wiltshire landowners, the Marquess of Lansdowne, as a means of abutting 'unjust charges'. After the first bill's failure at its second reading, a further measure made its way through Parliament, against a background of vitriolic abuse and recrimination. Young persistently referred to Anstie as 'the Wiltshire Woolman who has pushed himself forward',[17] and his *General View* as 'an unmeaning mass of error and deception'.[18]

A

LETTER

ADDRESSED TO

EDWARD PHELIPS, ESQ.

MEMBER FOR THE COUNTY OF SOMERSET;

CONTAINING

GENERAL OBSERVATIONS

ON THE

Advantages of Manufacturing the COMBING WOOL of ENGLAND, which is Smuggled to FRANCE;

AND

CURSORY REMARKS

ON THE

EVIDENCE given by the MANUFACTURERS to the COMMITTEE of the HOUSE of COMMONS:

ALSO,

A REFUTATION

OF THE

Argument adduced by the Author of the *Annals of Agriculture*, from an Official Paper of Monf. CALONNE;

TO SHEW

The Inconfiderable Quantity of BRITISH WOOL imported into FRANCE.

By the CHAIRMAN of the WOOL MEETING.

THE SECOND EDITION.

LONDON:

PRINTED BY STAFFORD AND DAVENPORT,

FOR J. DEBRETT, OPPOSITE OLD BOND STREET, PICCADILLY.

M.DCC.LXXXVIII.

Title page of John Anstie's pamphlet of 1788

The articulate Anstie described his opponents' objections as 'so ill expressed as to render the sense very obscure',[19] and accused Young of 'deforming his page with indiscriminate invective'. With delicate sarcasm he added, 'I find I was much mistaken in supposing that *The Annals of Agriculture* were generally read.'[20]

This controversy is an interesting illustration not only of the manufacturers' growing Parliamentary influence but also of the latent hostility between landed and manufacturing interests in a changing economic and political world. Sir Joseph Banks asked, 'Are the manufacturers to turn legislators?' This he thought was a threat to an Englishman's freedom. If a bill was wanted, it should be brought in by the Government and not by the manufacturers, and 'Justice ought to be done to the landed interest.'[21] Arthur Young's jibe that the manufacturers were inspired by 'the arithmetic of the counter, the policy of the shop' concealed a deeper social prejudice, which Anstie found both hurtful and bewildering, confessing that when he first saw volume 36 of *The Annals of Agriculture*, he was 'really mortified'. He did not view the bill in the light of 'opposition to the landed interest' but was fully convinced that both interests were inseparably united. In his pamphlets he tried to show that the increasing home and export trade required a plentiful supply of English wool in order to compete with other nations, and that the bill was inspired by no other motive than national prosperity.

> Your Lordship is too well acquainted with my general principles to suppose that I can be an advocate for unnecessary restrictions on trade. It is impossible for me to approve of any measure that may bear hard on a particular class of men, without examining with the utmost attention how far they are necessary to the public good.

Nevertheless he had been 'held forth to view as a person who is endeavouring to forge chains for binding the landowners and wool growers and as a promoter of regulations which a Turkish

Basha would be ashamed of'. The accusations of deception and prejudice he found particularly wounding:

> Though it evinces but little magnanimity of mind to be affected by every idle cavil that may be advanced against a person engaged in a public measure, yet I cannot be wholly insensible to those repeated efforts . . . to render myself and those persons with whom I am concerned obnoxious to the landowners and wool growers – I really believe it would be difficult to find any set of men less influenced by private views than those persons who compose the General Meeting in London.

He himself had tried to be 'unbiassed and attentive to what shall appear of public benefit'.[22]

Meanwhile he was so actively involved in giving evidence to Parliament and in preparation of the legislative details, that the bill became known at Westminster as 'Mr Anstie's Hobby Horse'.[23] Clearly he had established a complex information network. Returns of wool seized in 1786 and 1787 were delivered to him from the Customs by direction of the Treasury (see Table 1 opposite).

From the special fund set up by the General Wool Meeting he paid an agent to 'pass along the French coast', and obtain proof of the quantities of wool smuggled into France, which was submitted to Parliament in tabular form.[24] Anstie confessed:

> Had I enjoyed more leisure I should have gone to France myself which in all probability would have enabled me to have obtained more information.

The agent also 'found means to prevail on a Customs House officer' to secure details of wool imports, copies of which were regularly sent to Anstie 'with the French postmarks on them'.[25] During the five-week mission information was obtained from four ports – St. Malo, Port of Legue, Granville and St. Valery – and other smaller Normandy harbours (see Table 2 overleaf).

TABLE 1

QUANTITIES OF WOOL SEIZED AT VARIOUS PORTS IN 1786 AND 1787 (lbs.)

	1786	*1787*
Carlisle	–	3,341
Dover	–	385
Faversham	988	–
Folkestone	1,109	402
Hastings	2,129	2,440
Ipswich	326	–
Liverpool	1,022	–
London	686	2,404
Penzance	120	–
Portsmouth	61	
Rochester	–	409
Rye	1,404	–
Truro	1,889	–
Ulverstone	278	–
Whitby	59	–
Total	10,071	9,381

Source: *J.H.C.*, vol. 43, p. 285.

TABLE 2

ILLICIT IMPORTS OF BRITISH WOOL INTO FRENCH HARBOURS (lbs.)

	1783	*1784*	*1785*	*1786*
St. Malo	127,578	109,493	125,608	123,626
Port of Legue	100,494	132,436	87,627	67,854
Granville	–	–	–	201,859
St. Valery	–	–	–	159,571
Total	228,072	241,929	213,235	552,910

Source: *J.H.L.* Main Papers. Wool Bill Evidence, 9 June 1788.

Anstie received details of French manufactures in the Elbouef, Abbeville and Louviers workshops, where blue and grey riding cloaks were made, and also samples and prices of French goods and fleeces, so that he could compare quality and methods and discover how the French were outmanoeuvring their English competitors by mixing strong English combing wool with coarser French wool, contrary to his initial conceptions:

> This testimony is in direct contradiction to the original opinion that I myself had formed as a manufacturer of British short wool, and nothing but the Strictest Examination into these circumstances that came to my knowledge would have led me to believe that this was Practical.

He cited letters from well-known French merchants expressing a desire to purchase wool used in the manufactures of Halifax, Leeds, Exeter and Norwich – 'I know the handwriting of one of them', and marshalled corroborative evidence from other witnesses. Jacob Thomas Speidel, a Blackwell Hall factor, had seen smuggling of fleeces and flocks into Boulogne, and Captain John Sharpe described smuggling from Essex and Kent in vessels which brought back tobacco and spirits purchased with the illicit profits. Thomas Harvey of Penryn had written to Anstie, hoping for a reward for apprehending some smugglers – 'I hope I shall hear from you by the Return of Post how to proceed' – and asking that the officers wounded in the scuffle 'will receive some mark of your approbation'. Evidence taken before Yorkshire and Lincolnshire J.P.s revealed that wool was also being smuggled to Sweden. The testimony of other witnesses was 'entered in the Books of Mr Anstie', who had played a major role in assembling the evidence and was himself examined at great length in committee.[26]

In 1788 *The Salisbury Journal* reported that 'by the evidence of Mr Anstie of Devizes and of Mr Charles Clapham of Leeds it appears that upwards of 13,000 packs of wool are annually smuggled into France'.[27] Opponents of the bill

> endeavoured to lessen the force of the evidence which Mr. Anstie produced, alleging it not admissible unless the parties who procured the information were given up to be examined; but from Mr. Anstie's firmness and on his declaring that a person high in office had informed him that it would not be necessary to bring forward the persons concerned, and being supported by Mr. Wyndham, Mr. Hussey and other members, the gentlemen in the Opposition thought proper to yield.[28]

On 10 December 1787 *The Salisbury Journal* reported:

> Tuesday. A meeting of the principal persons in the Woollen Manufactories was held at the Minister's at Downing Street, Westminster: Mr Anstie of Devizes from the Committee of the Western Counties and Mr Patterson from the Norwich Committee attended and gave much information. It was agreed to ask leave of Parliament to bring in a bill to prevent smuggling of wool out of England.

The bill became law the following year, and included stringent regulations to make its provisions more effective.[29] It was a

276 *5° Martii.* *A.* 1788.

Report on Laws for preventing the Exportation of Sheep, Wool, &c. &c.

Your Committee having thought it expedient to enquire, by Examination of Witnesses, how far the Powers of the said Acts have operated to prevent or punish the several Offences therein enumerated, they called *John Anstie*, Esquire, Mr. *John Sharpe*, Mr. *John Cooper*, Mr. *Charles Clapham*, Mr. *Jacob Thomas Speidel*, and Mr. *Thomas Barnes*, whose respective Examinations and Evidence are as follow:

John Anstie, Esquire, examined.

How long have you acted as Chairman of the Wool Meeting?

I have acted as Chairman of the General Meeting from *April* 1786.

Had you any Meeting in the Country previous to the General Meeting in *London?*

We had—the First Meeting was held at *Bristol* in *September* 1784.

Did you attend a Wool Meeting in *Exeter* in 1786?

No.

Were the Resolutions of that Meeting printed?

They were.

Are the Conveniences of smuggling Wool from *Scotland* equal to those from *England?*

I am not competent to answer that Question, not being acquainted with that Coast.

On what Grounds did the Manufacturers at first begin their Enquiries?

They began their Enquiries on the Information of some Manufacturers in the County of *Somerset* respecting the smuggling of Wool and Live Sheep.

What Steps were taken in consequence of the Information received?

At the Second Meeting of the Manufacturers, the Evidence respecting the smuggling of Wool and Live Sheep appearing to warrant the Manufacturers Suspicions, they agreed to present a Memorial to the Lords of the Treasury, praying that a strict and vigilant Attendance might be given by the Officers of the Customs for preventing the Exportation of Wool and Live Sheep.

What occasioned the General Meeting in *London?*

I received Letters from the Manufacturers at *Exeter*, and also from the Wool Dealers in *Kent*, proposing a General Meeting in *London*, in order to apply to Parliament for an Amendment, or a total Repeal, of the present Laws for preventing the smuggling of Wool and Live Sheep.

What were the Dates of the Letters you received from *Exeter?*

Some Time about the End of *February* 1786.

From the Proofs in your Possession, and other Circumstances that have come to your Knowledge, are you persuaded that very considerable Quantities of *British* Wool are smuggled into *France* and other Foreign Parts?

From a strict and diligent Enquiry, I am now fully convinced not only of the Existence of the smuggling of Wool and Live Sheep, but also that a very considerable Quantity of Wool, and a great Number of Live Sheep, are constantly sent out of the Kingdom to *France* and other Foreign Parts.

Are you persuaded that any Wool is smuggled from *Scotland* to *France* or other Countries?

I am not fully persuaded, from any Information that I have received, which will warrant me to give such Information as I would wish to do upon every Occasion to this Committee.

Will you give the Committee a particular Account of the Proofs you are possessed of respecting the Exportation of Wool from *England?*

I would wish to divide the Information I have to give into Three distinct Parts.

The First Part consists of the Report from the Committee of this House in 1786, to which I beg Leave to refer.

The Second consists of a Return of Wool seized in the Years 1786 and 1787, as delivered to me from the Customs by the Direction of the Treasury; also of a Letter from *Penryn*, giving an Account of a Seizure of Worsted Yarn; and also an Account of Seizures that I have received in consequence of Letters that have been written to me. An Account of One Seizure I received from Mr. *Cooper*, Master of the *Saint Clement's* Coffee House, in the *Strand*, in the Year 1785, who told me, that a Vessel which sailed from *Birnham*, on the Coast of *Essex*, was brought into *Margate*, and there condemned: She had on board about 33 Cwt. of Wool, and was in Company with Seven other Vessels, all laden with Wool. This Information was also transmitted to me by Mr. *Everitt*, a *Blackwell Hall* Factor.

How were the other Vessels known to be laden with Wool, and why were they not seized?

The Master of the Vessel that was seized gave Information to Mr. *Cooper* who was then Surveyor of the Port of *Margate*, that Seven other Vessels had actually sailed in Company with him, at that Time loaded with Wool.—I know this only from the Account received from Mr. *Cooper*.

Do you know what became of those Seven Vessels upon their Return to this Country, after they had carried their Wool to the Coast of *France* or elsewhere?

I cannot say.

Don't you know, that upon the Information of the Captain who was seized, that those Vessels upon their Return were forfeited?

I do not.—I don't know that any such Law exists.

Did you make any Enquiry what became of those Vessels?

No; I did not.

—My Proof of the Third Part consists of an Account, containing the Information which I have obtained respecting the Quantities of *British* Wool imported into *France*, in consequence of having employed a Person to pass along the whole Coast of *France* on those particular Discoveries; and also, of Letters that I have seen, and which I believe to come from the Persons whose Names they bear—I know the Hand Writing of one of them. The Information they contain is to this Purport: "They express a strong Desire of forming "a Connection with the Person to whom they are "addressed, respecting the Purchase of *British* Wool "made use of in the Manufactures of *Halifax*, *Leeds*, "*Exeter*, and *Norwich*; and one of them engages to "take such Kind of Wool, without any Limitation of "Quantity, and pointing out Places where it may be "delivered at in *France*."—The Letters were written in the Years 1786 and 1787.

The Witness then produced—An Account of the Quantities of Wool seized in the Years 1786 and 1787, specifying the Places at which the same were seized [*Vide Appendix*, N° 1.] and also,

A Letter from Mr. *Thomas Harvey*, dated *Penryn*, *May* the 23d, 1786, to *John Anstie*, Esquire, *Devizes*, with a Postscript signed by *John Stona*, [*Vide Appendix*, N° 2.] and also,

A Table of the Importation of Wool in the Town of *Saint Malo*, from the 1st of *February* 1783

Extract from John Anstie's evidence to the House of Commons Committee in 1788

considerable achievement in the face of massed opposition from landowners and wool growers. Anstie admitted that he had experienced 'so much trouble in this difficult undertaking'.[30] The clothiers were delighted with his efforts. On 17 March 1788 the Wool Committee expressed their appreciation of 'the great attention of the Chairman to promote the interests and desires of the manufacturers'.[31] A Trowbridge clothier wrote: 'Mr Anstie has shown so much zeal, ability and real knowledge that he deserves attention and the heartfelt thanks of the Kingdom.'[32] As a token of their esteem, the Bath and West Society elected him Vice-President at their annual meeting on 11 December 1787.[33]

The export controversy established Anstie as an authority on wool and brought him into contact with members of Parliament and the Government. It was natural therefore that he should be used as a communication channel when ministers wished to consult manufacturers on the proposals for removing trade barriers with France and Ireland in the years 1784 to 1786. Pitt's encouragement of English trade and manufactures by a reduction of fiscal restrictions heralded a long period of English commercial and industrial ascendancy, and Anstie made a significant contribution to the implementation of this policy. Despite having 'neither at present nor any expectation or desire of being connected with the Irish trade',[34] he was interviewed by the Committee of Trade and Plantations on 8 February 1785,[35] an indication of his status and importance. The recent decrease in cloth exports to Ireland he attributed to Irish trade barriers and expressed confidence in the ability of English fine cloth to withstand competition, though Irish coarser cloth might enjoy a price advantage through the cheapness of the labour involved. He was also used by the Government as a publicist in promoting support for the policy, referring to his 'examination of the merits of the Irish propositions' and 'some of the official papers which were transmitted to me'.[36] Despite the opening of his factory, with which his time was 'at present very much taken up', he had been 'induced to give some liberty to his thoughts on this interesting subject'. Personally convinced that the Irish Treaty would benefit the English woollen trade, he sought to allay the Western manufacturers' fears. On 4 April he distributed copies of the Irish proposals, sent to him by the Secretary of the London Chamber of Commerce, to clothiers at Salisbury wool market and addressed a meeting of the Western manufacturers in Salisbury Council Chamber,[37] reading a letter from the Secretary to the Treasury, George Rose, and producing ministerial papers (see below, Table 3).[38]

TABLE 3

VALUE OF GOODS EXPORTED FROM ENGLAND TO IRELAND, SUBMITTED BY ANSTIE TO THE SALISBURY MANUFACTURERS 1785

	1781	*1784*
Coaches	£2,690 6*s*. 8*d*.	£5,140
Earthenware and Chinaware	£13,552 19*s*. 8*d*.	£15,322 17*s*. 4*d*.
Gloves	864 pairs	1,036 pairs
Gold and Silver Lace	32 lbs. 1 oz.	63 lbs.
Linen, Cotton and Silk Manufacture	£79,419 4*s*. 1*d*.	£113,027 12*s*. 9*d*.
Pictures	£520	£1,238 10*s*. 11*d*.
Silk Stockings	431 pairs	786 pairs
Wearing Apparel	£302 8*s*. 6*d*.	£1,010 16*s*. 10*d*.

Source: *S.J.*, 9 May 1785.

His allusion to 'the inconvenience he was subjected to'[39] shows that persuading the manufacturers of the merits of Free Trade was no easy task. The clothiers were suspicious of official manipulation, but Anstie as Chairman was careful to be completely impartial and to give all views a fair hearing:

> Several gentlemen thought the Chairman took unnecessary pains, but he declared that he wished to proceed with the greatest caution.

Armed with detailed trade statistics and 'all the papers that have been laid before Parliament', he canvassed opinions widely and formed his judgement by 'an impartial examination, free from prejudice and unbiassed by mere declamation':

> Nothing should be concealed that appears necessary to conviction – my object is not victory but truth'.[40]

Anstie later revealed that 'the principles which it was my object to inculcate have received almost general sanction',[41] and that for his part in 'explaining objections against those parts of the Irish propositions relevant to the woollen manufacture' he had been thanked 'by written communication from Government and it was acknowledged that he had rendered service to his native country', by winning support for the Irish Treaty, signed in 1785.[42] His attitude towards Ireland was objective, conciliatory and statesmanlike, in contrast to the views of many contemporary politicians. Anstie believed that:

> A permanent settlement with Ireland is for the mutual advantage of both Kingdoms.[43]

He showed an understanding of the past wrongs done to the Irish, and the need for maintaining amicable economic ties and promoting the real prosperity of Ireland:

> Although much has been done for Ireland, a part of it at least ought in every principle of justice to have been done long ago.

Anglo-Irish relations must not be soured by economic difficulties as they had been recently with America:

> By a prudent and temperate conduct it may be possible to alter them to the satisfaction of both countries without risking by an abrupt rejection of them another convulsion in the empire.[44]

Relationships in Europe could also be improved by closer trade links. Anstie's contacts in France and his investigations concerning the wool bill made him a valuable witness in the French negotiations. Sir Robert Peel the Elder, Matthew Boulton and Josiah Wedgwood were consulted among many others; Anstie was selected along with the Blackwell Hall factor, Thomas Everitt, to speak for the Western woollen manufacturers, being interviewed by a Committee of the Privy Council, including the French Treaty's architect, William Eden, on 10 February 1786. Many of the Superfine Cloth Manufacturers seemed apprehensive of French competition, but Anstie, as a Whig, was personally in favour of a less restricted economic policy. His evidence revealed a wide knowledge of French wool and manufacturing practice. He spoke of their cheaper labour, though he felt that, because of greater productivity, an Englishman earning 2*s*. a day might do his work more cheaply than a Frenchman at 1*s*. 6*d*. – 'I draw this inference from a Fact that has been related to me in a particular Manufacture.' He also believed that the French accommodated their goods to the foreign market better than English manufacturers.[45] He took his duties over this question seriously, procuring specimens of all the French woollen manufactures, and ascertaining their price, obviously having close contacts with the French trade. He mentioned a friend's book containing descriptions and illustrations of machines used by the French in the wool, cotton and silk manufactures in 1758,[46] and referred to 'information that I have been able to collect from a person just come from Paris, with whom my concerns are large', perhaps one of his numerous continental customers or agents.[47] During the negotiations he even allowed two French manufacturers to inspect 'his curious Manufactory' in Devizes to collect 'the most essential information of the best method of manufacturing his Superfine Cassimeres', a procedure disapproved of by many of his xenophobic contemporaries.[48] Anstie, however, favoured greater economic goodwill and a widening of the market, and he was convinced that the manufacturers of both kingdoms would derive advantage 'from an inspection of the Fabricks made in each country and as far as my own experience goes, a rivalship can never injure a manufacturer'. Free Trade with France, he felt, would benefit both British manufacturers and wool growers:

> Many years past I was informed by a person, who was then largely engaged in the exportation of woollens, that were a Free Trade opened to France, considerable quantities of our woollen goods would most certainly be introduced into that country. My own experience fully confirms this opinion, having been applied to by French woollen drapers for recommendations to manufacturers in this country for these kind of goods.[49]

Spain and Portugal, he thought, might be the next countries to be persuaded to lower their trade barriers: 'a considerable quantity of Salisbury Flannels are sent to Spain, notwithstanding their high duties – it is an article which the Spaniards cannot well do without'. He felt that it was 'of importance to open New Markets for our Goods' and fully supported the new liberal economic policy.[50] The French Treaty gave him great satisfaction:

> The philosophic mind cannot but view with pleasure two great and powerful nations, that have for a series of years exerted their utmost endeavours to destroy each other, now uniting with apparent cordiality, in promoting those measures which have a natural tendency to preserve the blessings of peace.[51]

Throughout his life, the quality and improvement of British wool was a subject of absorbing interest to Anstie. Anglo-French rivalry and the French Government's patronage of science and industry spurred British growers to try to improve the quality of native wool and to escape reliance on foreign supplies, which could be interrupted by war. For several centuries Spain had been the source of the finest wool available, much used in the West Country mixed with English short wool. Spanish Merino wool was so fine that a pound could be spun into 92 miles of yarn as opposed to 43 from a Lincoln. By 1750 Sweden, Saxony, Austria and France had broken through the protective barriers imposed on Spanish fine-wool sheep and had established their own Spanish flocks. The financial crisis after the loss of the American colonies made Britain aware of her dependence on the fine wool of Spain, imports of which cost £750,000 a year,[52] especially as the rapidity of enclosure and the concentration on meat rather than fleece in British flocks had coarsened local wool. Anstie himself wrote: 'The value of the fleece decreases nearly in proportion to the increased size and weight of the sheep.'[53]

In France, Professors Broussonet and D'Aubenton were conducting experiments in sheep breeding and management. From them in 1785 the President of the Royal Society, Sir Joseph Banks, whose London home had become a mecca for European savants, acquired a Spanish ram and ewe, which were the basis for his subsequent breeding experiments in Surrey and Middlesex. By 1788 he had helped George III to establish a Spanish Merino flock at Windsor, the King believing it to be 'a national object to improve the wool of this country'.[54]

John Anstie became curious about these experiments, and through a mutual friend, George Chalmers, Clerk to the Board of Trade, asked his old opponent over the wool bill if he could judge for himself how far the keeping of fine woollen sheep in England might be expected to succeed. In December 1790 Sir Joseph Banks sent two fleeces to Devizes by Clarke's waggon from *The White Swan*, Holborn Bridge, and asked for Anstie's opinion, 'as no one has a higher respect for your Judgement or your integrity than myself', a great compliment from a distinguished scientist. Anstie replied on New Year's Day, 1791. He did not think the fleece 'would prove equal to one of our Common Wiltshire Fleeces', but considered it to be 'in very good Condition as to the fineness of the wool – strong enough for combing – though it had probably coarsened through feeding on

English pastures'. Some had been scribbled and found to work freely and he proposed to make them into white cassimeres to facilitate comparison with the best Spanish wool. He was generally impressed with the quality and would embody his opinions in a letter to the Bath and West Society, a copy of which would be sent to Banks. Referring to their past differences, he concluded:

> I am much obliged to you for entertaining such favourable Sentiments respecting the rectitude of my Conduct. I have my own Opinion on the Commerce of Wool which is formed without attending to the prejudices of the two opposite parties. It will give me pleasure to see a spirit of liberality prevail which will prove to be for the mutual benefit of the Wool Growers and Manufacturers. My experience however has convinced me of the difficulty of effecting this with large Bodies of Men.

In conclusion, he wished Banks 'a happy recommencement of the New Year'.[55]

REFERENCES

1. British Museum (Sutro microfilm copies) IV. 7. 1–7. Report from H.C. Committee appointed to consider the Illicit Exportation of Wool, Live Sheep, Worsted and Yarn, 1786.
2. Anstie, *An Answer Addressed to Those who have read Sir John Dalrymple's Pamphlet in Support of a Tax and Permission to export raw wool* (1782), pp. 5–6, 23–4.
3. Anstie, *A General View of the Bill presented to Parliament during the last Session for preventing the illicit Exportation of British Wool and Live Sheep* (Bath, 1787), p. 9.
4. *S.J.*, vol. XLIX. 2413, 6 September 1784.
5. Anstie, *General View*, pp. 9–10.
6. H. Carter, *His Majesty's Spanish Flock* (1964), p. 40.
7. Anstie, *General View*, pp. 12–13.
8. H.L.R.O., *J.H.C.* vol. 43, p. 276.
9. Anstie, *A Letter Addressed to Edward Phelips Esq, on the Advantages of Manufacturing the Combing Wool of England, which is Smuggled to France* (1788), pp. 18–19.
10. Anstie, *General View*, pp. 21, 23, 29.
11. Anstie, *General View*, and *A Letter addressed to Edward Phelips*.

12. Anstie, *A Letter addressed to Edward Phelips*, pp. 2–3.
13. *Gentleman's Magazine*, 56 (1786), part 2, pp. 1137–8.
14. Anstie, *General View*, p. 76.
15. Letter of P. Milnes to Rev. Mr Beveridge, 14 October 1786. B.M. (SC) III.1.11–2.
16. Arthur Young, *The Annals of Agriculture*, vol. 7 (1786), p. 951.
17. Anstie, *General View*, pp. 135, 7, 123.
18. Young, op. cit., p. 95.
19. *Gentleman's Magazine*, 56 (1786), part 2, p. 1137.
20. Anstie, *General View*, pp. 133–4.
21. *The Annals of Agriculture*, vol. 9 (1788), pp. 493 and 502. Sir Joseph Banks, Instructions given to the Council against the Wool Bill.
22. Anstie, *General View*, pp. 135, 70, 34, 45, 101, 99, 103–4, 134.
23. Letter of William Davey to Lord Sheffield, 7 June 1787. B.M. (SC) III.6.43–4.
24. *J.H.C.*, vol. 43, p. 276.
25. Anstie, *General View*, pp. 100, 277.
26. H.L.R.O., Main Papers *J.H.L.*, p. 47. Evidence, 9 June 1788. *J.H.C.*, vol. 43, pp. 276–9, 279–83, 293.
27. W.A.S., W.C. 3, p. 113.
28. *S.J.*, vol. LII. 2545, 19 March 1787.
29. 28 George III. c. 38, 18 June 1788.
30. *Gentleman's Magazine*, 56 (1786), part 2, p. 1137.
31. Anstie, *Letter to Edward Phelips*, end page.
32. *B.C.* vol. XXVI. 1381, 10 May 1787.
33. *S.J.* vol. LII. 2585, 24 December 1787.
34. *S.J.* vol. L. 2448, 9 May 1785.
35. P.R.O. B.T. 6/106. Evidence for Irish Commercial Treaty.
36. Anstie, *General View*, p. 49.
37. Letter of Anstie to Henry Sweathman, 4 April 1785. B.L. Add. Mss. 22903.72.
38. *S.J.* vol. L. 2448, 9 May 1785.
39. P.R.O. B.T. 6/114. Evidence for French Commercial Treaty.
40. *S.J.* vol. L. 2445, 2447, 24482, 18 April, 2 May, 9 May 1785.
41. Anstie, *General View*, p. 130.
42. Anstie, *Observations*, p. 41.
43. *S.J.* vol. L. 2448, 9 May 1785.
44. B.L. Add. Mss. 22903.
45. P.R.O. B.T. 6/111 and 114. French Treaty correspondence.
46. Anstie, *Observations*, pp. 27, 29.
47. P.R.O. B.T. 6/114.
48. Letter of William Davey, Crediton manufacturer to Lord Sheffield, 7 June 1787, B.M. (SC) 6, pp. 43–4.

49. Anstie, *General View*, pp. 111, 97.
50. P.R.O. B.T. 6/114.
51. Anstie, *General View*, p. 111.
52. Patrick O'Brien, *Joseph Banks, a Life* (1987), p. 221.
53. Anstie, *An Answer*, p. 8.
54. Letter of His Majesty to Sir Joseph Banks, 29 November 1787. B.M. Banks Papers in Dawson Turner copies, V, p. 283.
55. Letters between John Anstie, Sir Joseph Banks and George Chalmers, Nov. 1790–Jan. 1791. B.M. (SC), I. 43–48.

CHAPTER THREE

John Anstie, Philanthropist, Citizen and Gentleman

Being also engaged in other concerns.

John Anstie, 1788

Despite his stature as a national figure, Anstie did not shrink from his civic responsibilities; he was closely connected with many local and provincial societies and left his mark on the social and religious life of the district. He had been christened in July 1746,[1] in a chapel at the back of a house in the Brittox where Baptists had worshipped for a century (see opposite).[2] Many leading townsmen, such as the Webbs, Bayntuns and Sir John Eyles M.P., had belonged to the congregation.[3] The Ansties figured prominently in the church's affairs, Richard and John the Elder acting as legacy trustees.[4] Church money was loaned to John and his widow, while their son, Benjamin, kept the accounts and was Chairman of the Building Committee of the Maryport Street Chapel, opened in 1780.[5] John Anstie (Jun.), seems to have become disenchanted with the Baptist Church. Since various ejected ministers had settled in Devizes after the Act of Uniformity, Presbyterians had worshipped in a chapel behind a house in Long Street, which had, however, recently collapsed. On 9 March 1790 John Anstie, George Hillier and Richard Knight leased a house and plot of ground called 'The Sampson' in Sheep Street,[6] and at the 1792 Quarter Sessions on 7 January, a certificate was registered for the newly erected Presbyterian chapel there, signed by Pastor Fenner, Anstie and

The original Baptist Chapel, Devizes

others.[7] In the same year nine Baptist members, including John's brother Benjamin, severed their connection with the chapel after an internal dispute and eventually joined the Presbyterians.[8] In 1797 John Anstie composed a letter inviting the Calvinist, James Biggs, to join them (see opposite) and this group later formed the nucleus of the New Baptist congregation.[9]

Despite his Nonconformity, Anstie was able to hold several civic offices through taking the Oath of Abjuration and Allegiance in the Court of Common Council on 24 December 1776. He acted as Grand Juror on 11 January 1790 in the case of Anne Raymond, who was sentenced to private whipping and six days' imprisonment.[10] From 1775 to 1777 he served as Overseer of the Poor for St. Mary's Parish, the second time voluntarily because of the parish's high rates and debts. A longer term of office, he felt, would achieve greater continuity and effectiveness, though business commitments had intervened, and he recognised that the work involved 'a great deal of drudgery'. One antidote to poverty was the Scribblers Club, a mutual benefit society for cloth workers in the town, established in 1765, of which Anstie was Treasurer in 1783. In a letter to the Secretary of the Bath and West Society, he outlined its usefulness in relieving the burden of the Poor Rate, providing for the indigent in sickness and death and in preserving the self-respect of the members, many of whom were probably his own employees.[11] He may also have been involved in running the Bridewell. At a meeting on 16 August 1786 of the Bridewell Committee, consisting 'of the principal Manufacturers and other Gentlemen', resolutions were passed on the exportation of wool, with which he was so closely concerned, and recommending a reduction in the number of alehouses.[12]

In 1771 Anstie joined the Bear Club, a social and philanthropic society founded in 1756, whose members included Henry Addington, later Lord Sidmouth, and Thomas Lawrence, father of the artist (see partial listing on p. 64).[13] An annual dinner was held in August with a 2*s*. 6*d*. fine for non-attendance; members paid an annual subscription of 2*s*. 6*d*.

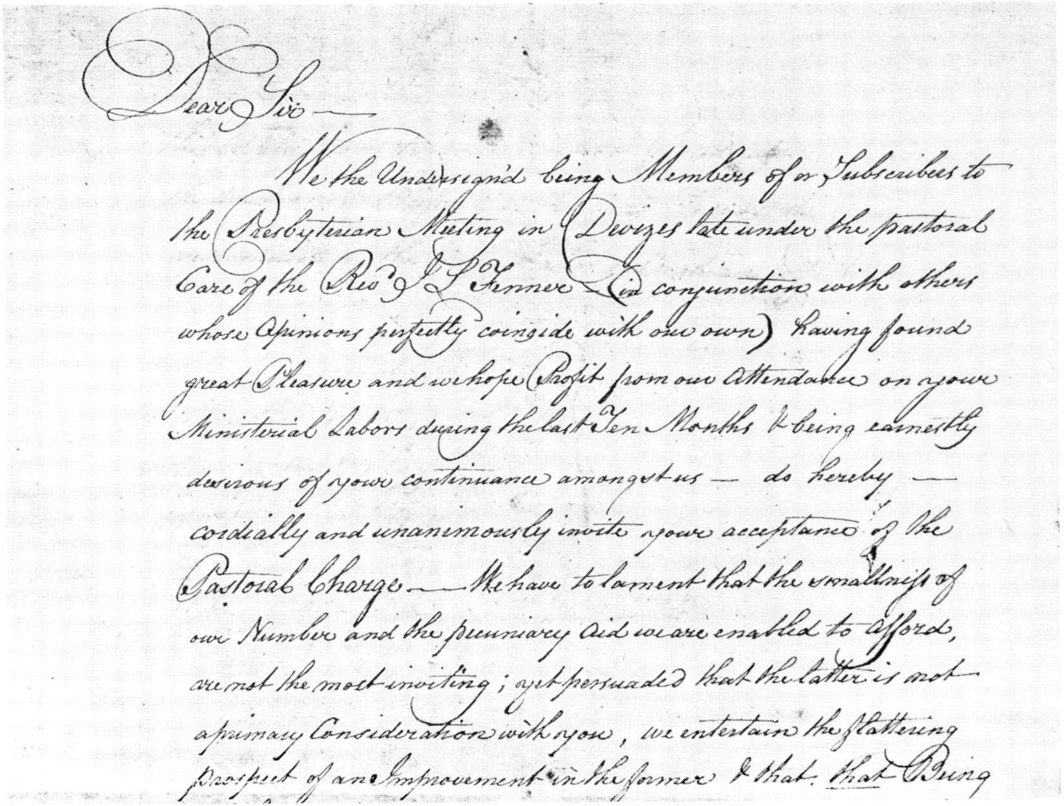
Dear Sir —

We the Undersign'd being Members of or Subscribers to the Presbyterian Meeting in Devizes late under the pastoral Care of the Revd J L Fenner (in conjunction with others whose Opinions perfectly coincide with our own) having found great Pleasure and we hope Profit from our Attendance on your Ministerial Labors during the last Ten Months & being earnestly desirous of your continuance amongst us — do hereby — cordially and unanimously invite your acceptance of the Pastoral Charge — We have to lament that the smallness of our Number and the pecuniary Aid we are enabled to afford, are not the most inviting; yet persuaded that the latter is not a primary Consideration with you, we entertain the flattering prospect of an Improvement in the former & that. that Being

Part of a letter written by John Anstie to the Reverend James Biggs in 1797

Members Names.

Mr. Samuel Beaven
John Tylee
Samuel Tayler
George Sloper
Edward Eyles, Eſq;
Mr. George Hillier
William Salmon
John Neate
William Clare
Robert Waylen
John Anſtie
Joſiah E. Heathcote, Eſq;
Rev. Edward Innes
Mr. Richard Maltby
Benjamin Sloper
Stephen Hillman
Robert Bruges
Stephen Powell
Doctor Barwis
Mr. James Gent
James Sutton, Sen. Eſq;
Mr. Richard Chandler

List of some of the members of the Bear Club in 1777

and 6*d.* to attend at *The Black Bear* every Tuesday night. At ten o'clock the 'reckoning' was called, absentees being fined 4*d.* From these funds a school was founded to educate sixteen town boys over ten for three years. Instruction in the three Rs was accompanied by moral education, particularly eschewing 'swearing and lying, the grand leaders to all other vices', and the boys were to show 'Respect to those whom they meet, particularly to those in stations or degrees above them'. The pupils attended church twice on Sunday, and were provided annually with coat, waistcoat, breeches and hat.[14] At the proper age they were apprenticed to a trade; in 1776 John Anstie (Sen.) took on Benjamin Garland, and his son employed Joseph Glass in his factory in 1788.[15] Anstie was elected to the committee in 1784, remaining a club member until 1802. He was fined for missing the annual dinner in 1794, 1795, 1799 and 1801. This was evidently a sumptuous affair, attended in 1816 by 'seventy gentlemen of the first rank and consequence', who consumed 'three bucks, two turtles and a profusion of every other delicacy, fruits and ices'; afterwards songs and glees were sung.[16]

The late eighteenth-century zeal for improvement, which produced schools and canals, enclosures and hospitals, also spawned Improvement Commissions, whose aim was to make the streets safer by providing lighting and paving and clearing away refuse. The co-opted members, usually the chief business inhabitants, sought to reinforce the principle of personal obligation which was the basis of English local government. Predictably Anstie was one of the ninety-seven trustees of the commission set up in Devizes in 1781, which met weekly at *The Black Bear* or *The Castle Inn*. Finance was provided from a 9*d*. in the pound rate and Sunday tolls from cattle and carriages passing into the town. Surveyors supervised the provision of amenities and a scavenger saw that the streets were kept clean. Four night watchmen patrolled the streets from 11 p.m. to 4 a.m., three watchboxes being erected at suitable points; ninety lamps were to be lit from dusk till 2 a.m. Residents who paved in front of their doors were allowed 2*s*. 6*d*. to defray the cost and handbills cautioned those who did not sweep the footways.

On 5 October 1782 Anstie's offer to perform the office of Scavenger in St. Mary's Parish at £21 a year was accepted as the lowest tender. The duties were defined as 'sweeping and cleansing the streets in a proper and sufficient manner and removing all the dung, manure and compost – twice in every week'. On 30 August 1783 he also proposed to light the lamps for the next eight months, at 10*d*. a lamp, which he did so conscientiously that on 17 July 1784 he was officially thanked for 'his great care, attention and punctuality in lighting the lamps and repairing the streets during the last year'. During the years 1785 to 1787, when he was immersed in the wool bill controversy and other national economic activities, Anstie performed the triple duties of surveyor, lamplighter and scavenger in St. Mary's Parish on a contractual basis, possibly employing paupers. Strict standards were enforced by the trustees. A lamplighter was

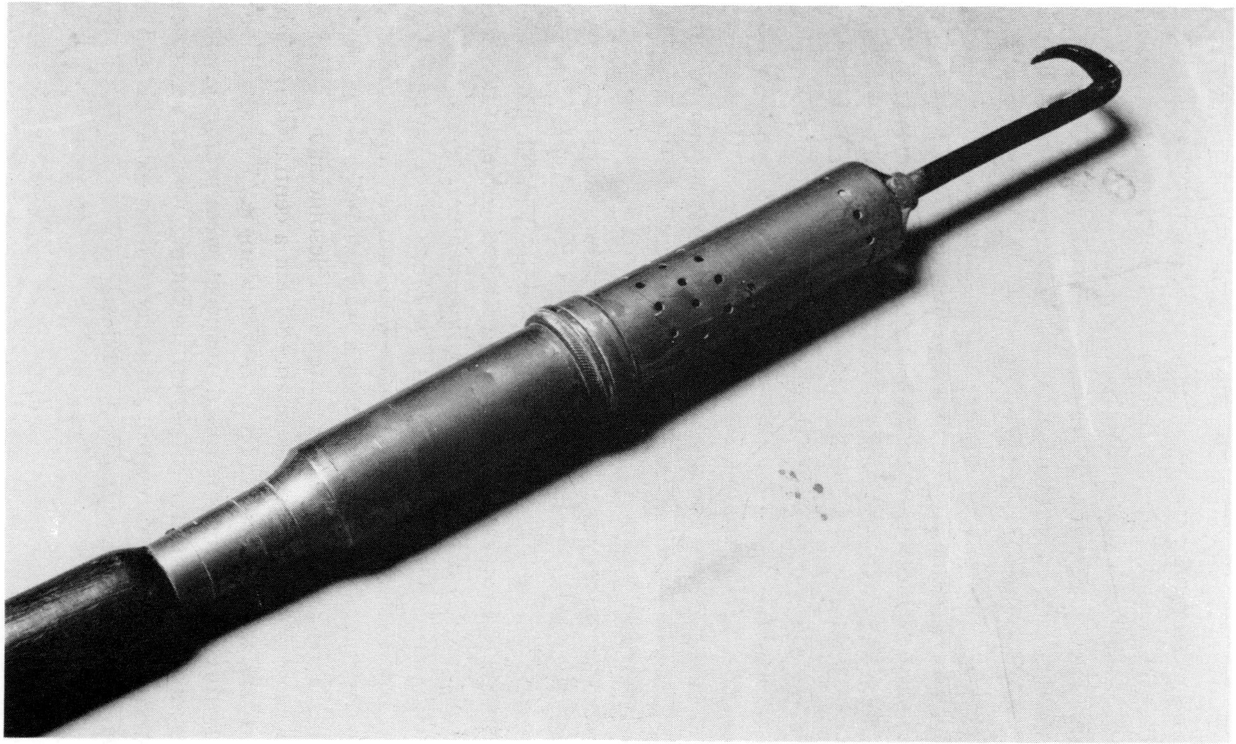

Anstie's lamplighter

prosecuted for failing in his duty and several watchmen were dismissed for misbehaviour, innkeepers being particularly asked 'not to harbour them'. A meeting on 15 August 1785, during Anstie's period as scavenger, condemned many inhabitants for carrying away, presumably for sale, 'great quantities of dung and soil without the approbation of the Scavenger – he is hereby directed to be particularly attentive in discovering such offenders'. There was evidently some vandalism, a 10*s*. reward being offered for information about damage to the lamps. The officials' accounts were carefully scrutinised; in March 1784, two St. Mary's surveyors, investigated by a committee of four, including Anstie, were found to be £3 14*s*. 0½*d*. short, and in 1790 Anstie's and Sloper's books did not balance by 8*s*. 5½*d*., but 'the same was immediately paid into the Treasurer's hands'. During the years 1789 to 1794 Anstie's attendance, particularly at daytime meetings, grew less frequent due to business pressure, and in 1794 he felt it necessary and honourable to resign after his bankruptcy.[17]

The last quarter of the eighteenth century also produced a large number of associations for the preservation of law and order, resulting from the inability of unpaid parish constables and ageing night watchmen to cope with an increase in crime. The Devizes Society for Prosecuting Felons originated at a meeting on 21 December 1787 at *The Black Swan*, attended by Anstie and other leading inhabitants, to consider how to protect their persons and property from a wave of petty crime. Individual legal proceedings were often troublesome and expensive, but successful prosecutions financed from a central fund might be a salutary deterrent. At a further meeting on 7 January 1788 sixty-three subscribers enrolled, many of them prominent businessmen. A committee of eleven, including Anstie, was given power to offer scaled rewards for successful prosecutions and to apprehend felons (see Table 4 overleaf).

TABLE 4

DEVIZES PROSECUTION SOCIETY

SCALE OF REWARDS FOR APPREHENSION OF CRIMES 1787

Burglary Highway Robbery Housebreaking Setting Fire to House Barn Outhouse Hay Corn Maiming or Stealing Cattle	£5 5*s*. 0*d*.
Receiving Stolen Goods Knowingly	£3 3*s*. 0*d*.
Stealing Poultry Corn Hay	£2 2*s*. 6*d*.
Cutting or Damaging Trees Stealing Wood Damaging Gates Hedges Rails Ironwork Stealing Fish from Pond Robbing Gardens or Orchards Pulling up Garden Stuff	10*s*. 6*d*.

Source: W.R.O. 1553/6
Devizes Prosecution Society Minute Book 1787–91.

Watchman's rattle

Borough members subscribed a minimum of 3*s*. 6*d*. and villagers 7*s*. 6*d*.; Anstie and his brother each contributed 10*s*. 6*d*. Any member robbed was to report the theft immediately to the Secretary and Treasurer.

During Anstie's period of office from 1788 to 1791, Robert Waylen's bay gelding was stolen from a field in Brick Kiln Lane and two unripe melons were filched from Mr Sedgefield's garden. In 1791 Anstie brought a case against one of his employees, Joseph Cole, who had stolen some fancy silk and wool waistcoats valued at 36*s*. from the factory. At the meeting on 16 December 1791 Anstie was allowed £10 14*s*. for expenses incurred in the prosecution.[18] Cole was convicted at Winchester Assizes[19] and Anstie was awarded a certificate exempting him from all Parish and Borough offices for apprehending a felon (see opposite).[20] On 1 March 1792 Anstie sold the ticket to John Rose for £10, which he donated to society funds.[21] He was also moved to secure the release of the offender:

> Joseph Cole, the youth who was condemned at our late Assizes for robbing his master, Mr Anstie of Devizes, owes his life and will most probably be indebted for his future happiness to the generosity and humanity of that gentleman, who, having vigilantly pursued the means of public justice to his conviction, there ceased the painful task of prosecuting and not only forgave him the injury he had done, but became his advocate, and interceding with the Judge, procured him his free pardon. After which, in the true spirit of philanthropy, he took him again under his protection, with a view to reclaim him and make him an honest and deserving member of society.[22]

Reform of another sort had earlier occupied Anstie's mind. Sharing the widespread unease at Government corruption and high wartime taxation, he attended the Wiltshire Reform Association meeting at Devizes on 26 January 1780, addressed by the Earl of Shelburne and Charles James Fox, the leading Lords and Commons Opposition spokesmen.[23] A petition was read, demanding the remedying of abuses in public expenditure and a committee established to support reform and co-operate with other counties. At a subsequent Devizes meeting on 28 March it was proposed to send a message of good wishes to Lord Shelburne for a speedy recovery from a recent duelling wound.[24] Despite his friendship with Shelburne, Anstie objected that this was a private matter and they should not seem to give public countenance to the practice of duelling, but he was overruled. He also unsuccessfully questioned a motion thanking the two Wiltshire M.P.s, Ambrose Goddard and Charles Penruddocke, for their independent conduct in the Commons, as in his view the latter sometimes voted with the Government; it seems that Anstie took a close interest in Parliamentary debates. On 6 April the Commons motion of John Dunning, M.P. for Calne, 'That the influence of the Crown has increased, is increasing and ought to be diminished' was passed, but soon disasters in America, the

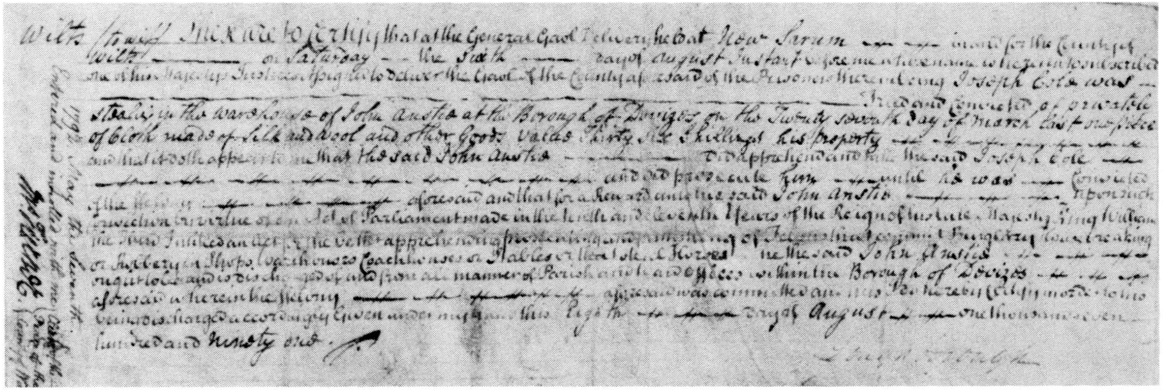

John Anstie's 'Tyburn Ticket', 1791 (W.A.S. Collection)

Gordon riots, and the French Revolution eroded support for reform and led to a wave of reactionary complacency. In 1788 the centenary of the Glorious Revolution was celebrated with a bonfire in Devizes Market Place,[25] and in the following year George III's recovery from illness was marked by a procession, dinner and entertainment at the Town Hall, followed by fireworks.[26] Anstie attended the meeting of 'The Association of the Friends to the King and Constitution' in Devizes on 13 December 1792 to express support for 'our happy Constitution . . . the pride and glory of Britons as well as the envy and admiration of the world'.[27] Anstie chaired a meeting of Protestant Dissenters in the town on 2 January 1793 which ratified his declaration expressing their 'unfeigned attachment to the Civic Constitution of Great Britain', a document which illustrates his moderate and liberal principles:

> Fully sensible that all human governments are necessarily subject to some degree of imperfection, they admire the Constitution of this country as possessing, by the essential principles on which it is formed, full and adequate energy to reform its own abuses, without being subject to those convulsions which are so inimical to the dictates of humanity. With particular pleasure they contemplate the blessings enjoyed by the inhabitants of this kingdom, and they sincerely wish to promote and enlarge the prevailing spirit of religious Liberty, by cultivating those principles of justice and moderation which alone can unite persons of different religious persuasions, and which . . . will be productive of complete national felicity. Conscious that it is in the interests as well as the duty of every person to promote general tranquillity, it is their earnest desire to assist the civil Magistrates in suppressing all tumults and disorders, and in enforcing obedience to the laws.

The meeting expressed thanks to the Chairman for his 'judicious attention and candid obliging conduct'.[28]

A month before, the tranquillity of Devizes had been disturbed by Canal Mania. At a meeting held on 12 December to consider 'the propriety of forming an inland communication' between Bristol and the Salisbury and Southampton Canal, which would be 'highly useful and beneficial to the public at large', Anstie was elected to the committee of twenty-one.[29] This scheme was originally intended to distract attention from the engrossing of the Kennet and Avon Canal shares by two Bristol lawyers and resulted in 'The Mad Gallop to Devizes', when 2,000 would-be subscribers descended on the town from Bristol, Somerset and Wiltshire in coaches, on horseback and even in a hearse.[30] A tent was erected in the Market Place to cope with the influx and the magistrates even considered reading the Riot Act. The event was commemorated in a long poem which ran through two editions in a fortnight. It begins:

> At fair Devizes' pleasant town
> An Ancient Borough of Renown
> Where Those who in Canal a share
> Would fain secure, must fast repair.

And later continues:

> For news unwelcome meets their ear
> Whereby they learn a different route
> For famed Canal is pointed out
> By which their wishes all are crossed
> And hopes of future winnings lost.[31]

By the time the sponsors were brought into the Kennet and Avon scheme in 1793, personal investment was impossible for Anstie.

For his own frequent journeys to London and Bath, and visits to such friends as Thomas Coke of Norfolk, Anstie possessed 'a neate phaeton for a pair or a single horse'.[32] During the 1780s he must have frequently travelled the Great West Road to and from London. On one occasion in 1788, when perhaps he was returning from a meeting on the wool bill, he was attacked outside Staines by three footpads, who stole two guineas and some silver from Anstie and a watch from his servant.[33] The Chapter Coffee House at 50 Paternoster Row was his London address and political base.[34] The vogue for coffee houses reached its zenith in the eighteenth century, when there were some 550 in London, divided on functional lines. The Chapter Coffee House was first mentioned in the *Daily Courant* in 1722, and came to be frequented by booksellers, writers and men of letters, 'chap' books deriving their name from the establishment. It was noted for its punch, pamphlets and good supply of English and French newspapers, and figured frequently in advertisements, indicating the wide range of activities centred there, such as a subscription library and a chemical society. It was obviously ideally suited to Anstie's political and literary interests. Eighteenth-century habitués included George Robinson, the bookseller, and the poets, Thomas Chatterton and Oliver Goldsmith.

Anstie also mixed with a cultured and cosmopolitan set in Bath. On 8 September 1777 a society was formed for 'the diffusion of useful information', calling itself The Bath and West of England Society for the Encouragement of Agriculture, Arts, Manufactures and Commerce.[35] It was addressed to 'Gentlemen of Public Character and Liberal Minds'[36] in 'this present age of liberal enquiry'.[37] Among founder members were the Marquess of Bath, Sir Richard Colt Hoare, Joseph Priestley and Thomas Davis, while the Inspector General of Manufactures in France and M. Konhoff, from Russia, sent to England to study agriculture by the Empress Catherine, were honorary members.[38] The society encouraged experiment and published papers on technical and agrarian subjects. The December annual meeting, preceded by a grand dinner, for which the Marquess of Ailesbury donated a doe in 1791, became famous 'for the resort of noblemen, gentlemen, farmers, manufacturers and artisans interested in various improvements'.[39]

At the first annual meeting on 9 December 1777, Anstie was elected to the society's Committee of Manufactures and Commerce, a testimony to his reputation in the area, eight years before he built his new factory and five years before the wool controversy. He took an active part in the work of the committee, which met on the third Tuesday of every month. Premiums were offered for inventions such as spinning jennies for fine cloth, waterproof boots and the use of oil in woollen manufacture. A carding machine and a device for lighting coal mines were examined and in 1784 Anstie reported on his trial of Mr. Hunt's

Scene in a coffee house. Etching by Thomas Rowlandson (1756–1827)

machine for drying cloth: 'it did not work properly on account of some imperfections in construction', which the inventor would have to remedy. He procured for the committee's inspection an original machine from the Devizes area, 'simple in its construction, and well adapted for Dispatch in slicing Turnips', which the society subsequently recommended.[40] His advocacy of the 'very considerable advantages' of Friendly Societies resulted in the society offering a prize for groups of over thirty members.[41] In 1787 he became a member of the Committee of Correspondence and Enquiry, which also chose books for the society's reference library, and a year later was elected a vice-president, largely as a reflection of his contribution to the passage of the wool bill.

During the years 1788 to 1791 Anstie was involved in disagreement with Dr. James Anderson, a vice-president of the society. He read Anderson's accounts of the work of the Northern Society for the Improvement of British Wool with some scepticism, wishing to have a fleece of Highland wool for inspection, and submitting his own 'strictures on the subject' to the Committee of Manufactures and Commerce. The Secretary tried to reconcile the two men, but received the discouraging reply on 8 September 1788 that 'Mr Anstie's private engagements will not for the present admit of his corresponding as proposed with Dr. Anderson on the subject of wool.' At the annual meeting on 14 December 1790 papers from both men were read and 'well received', and the following year Anstie published his views in the form of a letter to the Secretary of the Bath and West Society, 'to be distributed among my friends' and 'to excite a general interest among the manufacturers'.[42]

He challenged Anderson on two points, the suggested substitution of Highland for Spanish wool in fine-cloth manufacture and the assertion that the wool export ban had caused the deterioration of local wool. Anstie maintained that the increasing 'demand in the home market for fine goods, owing to our riches' required rather an increase in Spanish wool imports. The coarsening of English wool during the last forty years he attributed to enclosures, the introduction of turnips and artificial grasses and the concentration on size rather than fleece:

> One particular sort of fine wool which I formerly purchased and which grew on the sheep kept on heaths and commons, seems to be wholly lost.

Soil and pasture, he thought, were vital factors in wool quality. He cited the example of 'a person not many miles from Devizes who possesses a small tract of down where the soil is particularly fine; he considers this ground to be particularly adapted for raising fine wool'. He continued:

> If our wool has been debased by the causes I have assigned, it may be impracticable ever to restore it to its original quality without an entire change of our system of agriculture, which I suppose no person will think desirable merely to obtain a finer growth of wool.

He suggested the society might offer prizes for the finest wool from sheep fed on enclosures,[43] and for discovering the plants most agreeable to sheep.[44]

He was by now regarded as a wool expert, and on 14 June 1791 was appointed to a special committee of the Bath and West Society to examine two sheep from different farmers for the relative quality of their fleece and meat, being later thanked by the Secretary for 'his obliging attention to South Down wool'. After his bankruptcy he remained an honorary and corresponding member and was kept informed of society meetings. He was probably consulted on wool matters, as the Secretary's correspondence records include 'sending goods to John Anstie of Rowd' on 21 May 1795, and an invitation to the Wool Committee on 16 July 1796. Later that year he wrote to the Secretary, asking for financial help in patenting a small spinning-machine for children. Matthews replied:

> The Society will hear with pleasure of any success in your project, but your Idea of getting a Patent, if realized, will throw the object out of the province of this Society with regard to the Premium; any further Information from you on this or any other Topic will be received with pleasure by the Society.[45]

Anstie's mechanical and scientific interests are also reflected in his possession of 'a patent copying machine',[46] 'a neat electrifying machine with apparatus, a reflecting telescope brass-mounted and two twelve inch globes'.[47] These gadgets were perhaps acquired through his London and Bath contacts.

The New Park Street house (see below) to which Anstie took his bride, Mary Vesey of Wotton-under-Edge, in 1780, was sold on 29 July to him and his brother Peter by Robert Nicholas, M.P. for Cricklade, when it was described as 'a messuage or tenement, with the coach house, barn, stables, outhouses, garden and orchard'.[48] Traces of the original fifteenth-century gabled and timber-framed house remain, but the house was refronted in the early seventeenth century and in the late eighteenth century given a plain Bath stone Georgian front, and

John Anstie's house in Devizes

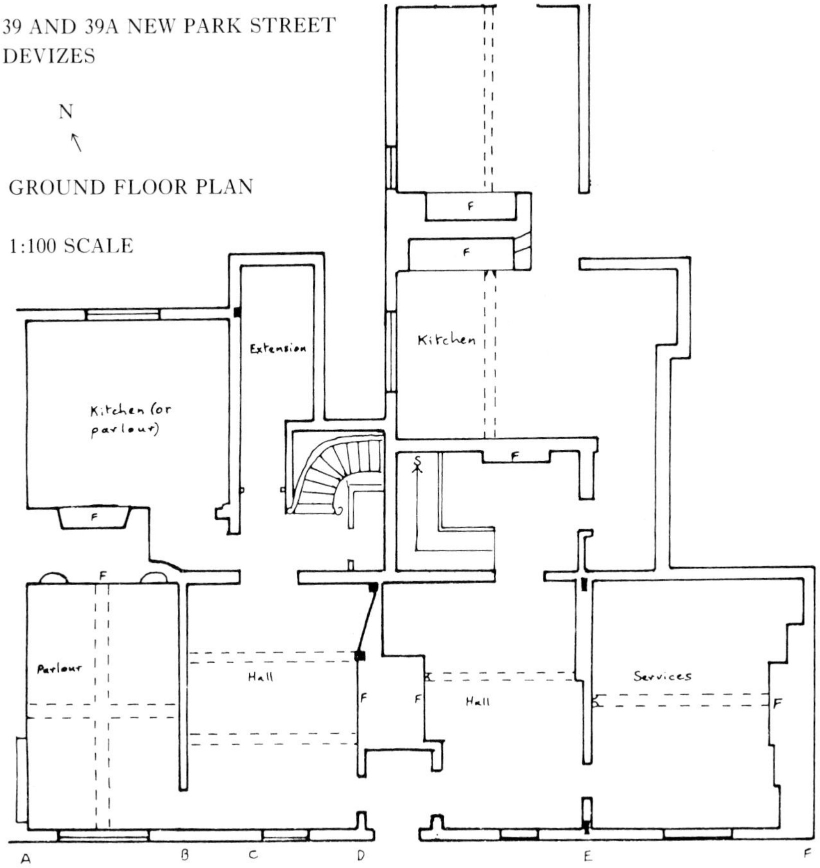

Plan of John Anstie's house (from Wiltshire Buildings Record survey, 1982)

a porch with two stone Doric columns. The ground floor contained the old mediaeval hall, with a parlour and service rooms, and first-floor chambers over (see above). Some fine eighteenth-century features include a classical archway, a walnut inlaid stair rail and plaster ceiling motif and cornice (see pp. 81 and 82).[49] The auction list of Anstie's household effects in 1794 also illustrates his elegant and tasteful standard of living, and suggests a considerable degree of comfort and hospitality.

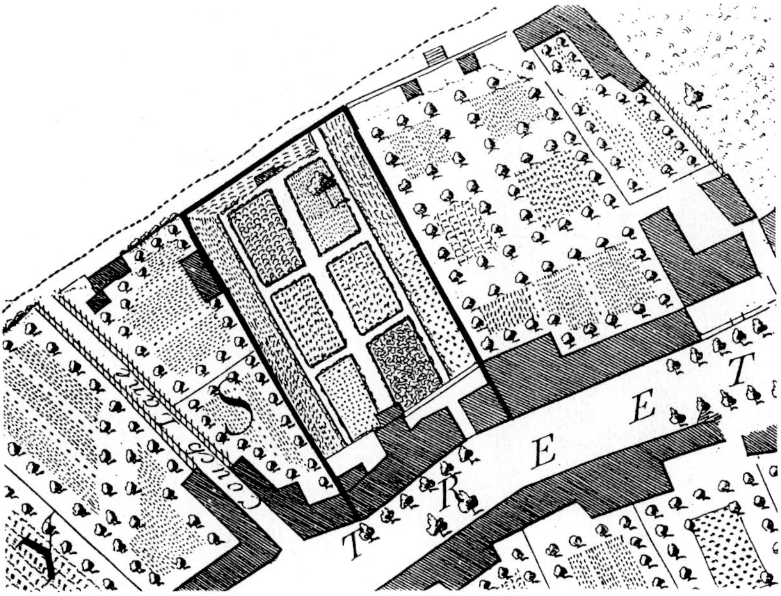

Plan of the garden of Anstie's house in 1759 (Edward Dore's map)

> A general assortment of mahogany furniture, a very complete circular sideboard table, a neat wardrobe and bookcase, eight neat japaned dining room chairs, an eight day clock in mahogany case, bedsteads with cotton and other furniture, good beds and bedding, about 300 oz of modern plate, table and tea china . . . a few books, one pipe of port wine in cask, about 20 dozen of claret etc, brewing furnace and utensils, several iron bound hogsheads and two hogshead casks.[50]

Edward Dore's map of 1759 shows a formally laid out garden behind the house, a stable and a carriage way to the east leading into Back Lane, now Commercial Road (see above). An interest in gardening is suggested by Anstie's stewarding of the Trowbridge Carnation Feast on 25 July 1781.[51] A letter to the *Wiltshire Gazette* dated 9 October 1905, before the area was redeveloped, described the nearby courts of working-class cottages, each with a patch of garden, which probably housed some of the factory workmen.[52]

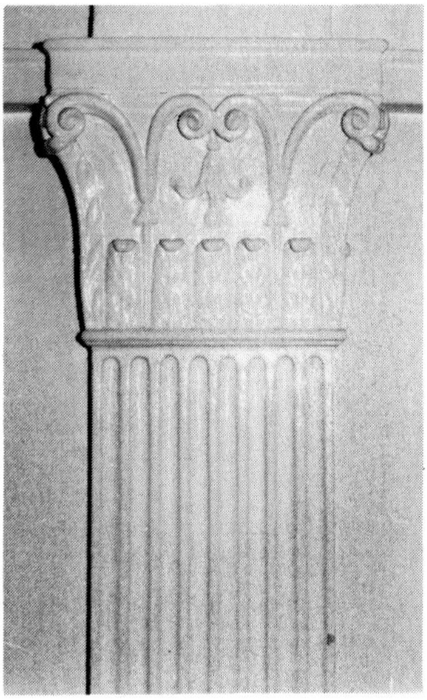

The hallway arch, an arch detail, and the wall oven in John Anstie's house in Devizes

A staircase curtail and plaster ceiling motif in John Anstie's house

Anstie's elegant house was appropriate to his status. He appeared as one of the principal gentry of Wiltshire in a 1791 survey[53] and mixed easily with county society, referring to 'the solid advantages' which he derived from personal conversation with the Marquess of Lansdowne,[54] who owned a Devizes town house as well as being a fellow member of the Bath and West Society. He spoke of visiting Lord Liverpool, by whom he had been 'much noticed',[55] and knew many leading contemporary figures, such as Richard Arkwright and Thomas Coke of Norfolk.[56] Cosmopolitan contacts included 'a person of credit who has been in Spain'[57] and 'a friend of mine who resided some time in Constantinople'.[58] Like most eighteenth-century gentlemen, he took snuff, using an oval gilt snuffbox with a pebble in the lid, perhaps one of the famous Bromham quartz pebbles, and, if so, a reminder of the family's origin.[59]

Anstie's contacts and publications show him to have been a man of some culture and refinement. His intellectual abilities suggest that he was not just the product of a local charity school. He may have been educated at the Bratton School run by Jeffery Whitaker between 1725 and 1777, which many local Dissenting tradesmen's sons attended and where Latin, English, Penmanship, Arithmetic, Merchants' Accounts, Geometry, Use of the Globes, Drawing and Surveying were taught.[60] In his pamphlets he shows a good grasp of general historical developments, referring to reading 'some ancient English historian', and surveying economic progress in France since Louis XIV's reign. He had a wide knowledge of European economic affairs[61] and had critically read Adam Smith's *Wealth of Nations*.[62] He appeared as a subscriber to a book published in Devizes in 1773, and now in W.A.S. Library, entitled *The Way to the Temple of True Honour and Fame by the Paths of Heroic Virtue*. His literary style was lucid and cultured, and though prone to aphorism, using such phrases as 'Home is Home, though ever so homely,'[63] he wished to 'strip every question of all unnecessary appendages and reduce it to as simple a form as possible', and to 'express my thoughts with perspecuity'.[64] The pseudonym chosen for his earliest pamphlet, 'A Plain Matter of Fact Man',[65] suggests the candour and altruism which pervaded his participation in local affairs.

REFERENCES

1. W.R.O., 1215/6. Baptist Account Book 1729–92.
2. *V.C.H. Wiltshire*, vol. 3, pp. 108–9.
3. W.A.S., W.C. 6, pp. 50–1.
4. W.R.O., 1215/6.
5. W.A.S., W.C. 6, pp. 50–1.
6. W.R.O., 1270/6. Devizes land deeds, 1742–1837.
7. B. Cunnington, *Annals of the Borough of Devizes*, 2 vols., vol. 2, 1791–1830, p. 206.
8. W.R.O., 1215/2. Baptist Minute Books, 1818–40.
9. W.A.S., J. Waylen, *Nonconformity in Devizes* 13, n.p.
10. W.R.O., A2/150/2. Devizes Borough Sessions records, 1790–1819.
11. Letter of John Anstie to the Secretary, 1 November 1783. *Letters and Papers of the Bath and West of England Society*, vol. 3, pp. 350–1. Anstie's connection with the Bath and West Society is dealt with more fully later in this chapter.
12. W.A.S., W.C. 3, p. 37, *S.J.*, August 1786.
13. W.R.O., 1090/2. Bear Club accounts book, 1775–9.
14. W.A.S., *W.T. 27*, (11a), pp. 7, 8–10. Bear Club rules.
15. W.R.O. 1090/2.
16. W.A.S., c./5/27.
17. W.R.O., G20/5/3–4. Improvement Commission Minute Books, 1781–96.
18. W.R.O., 1553/6. Devizes Prosecution Society Minute Book, 1787–91.
19. *S.J.* vol. LVI. 2774, 8 August 1791.
20. W.A.S., Devizes Mss. 1. This was popularly known as a Tyburn Ticket, originating in an Act of 1699 'for the better apprehension of felons in robbing shops, warehouses, coach houses and stables'.
21. W.R.O., 1553/6.
22. *S.J.* vol. LVI. 2776, 22 August 1791.
23. W.A.S., *W.T.* 12 (6). Proceedings of the Reform meeting 1780.

24. J. Waylen, *A History Military and Municipal of the Ancient Borough of Devizes* (Devizes, 1859), p. 441.
25. J. Waylen and C. Gillman, *Annals of Devizes* (Devizes, 1908), p. 21.
26. W.A.S., W.C. 3, p. 118.
27. *S.J.* vol. LVII. 2845, 17 December 1792.
28. *S.J.* vol. LVIII. 2849, 14 January 1793.
29. *S.J.* 17 December 1792.
30. Waylen, *History of Devizes*, p. 468.
31. W.A.S., *W.T.* 37, (3), Romaine Joseph Thorn, *The Mad Gallop to Devizes* (1793).
32. *S.J.*, vol. LIX. 2933, 25 August 1794.
33. W.C. 24, p. 49.
34. P.R.O., B.T. 6/111. French Treaty correspondence.
35. *Letters and Papers, Bath and West Society*, vol. I, p. vi.
36. Bath R.O., Bath & West Journal 1/2, 1777–91.
37. *Letters and Papers, Bath and West Society*, vol. IV, p. xv.
38. Bath R.O., Bath & West Journal 1/2.
39. Warner, Rev. R., *History of Bath* (Bath 1801), p. 314.
40. B.R.O., Bath & West Journal 1/2.
41. *Letters and Papers, Bath and West Society*, vol. IV, p. 176.
42. Bath R.O., Bath & West Journal 1/2.
43. Anstie, *Letter to the Secretary of the Bath and West Society*, Introduction, p. v, and pp. 5, 17, 21, 19–20, 24, 28.
44. *Gentleman's Magazine*, vol. 61, pt. 1, p. 516.
45. B.R.O., Letters and Minutes of the Bath and West Society, 1/3.
46. *B.H.*, vol. IV, 150, 10 Jan. 1795.
47. *S.J.* vol. LIX. 2933, 25 August 1794.
48. W.C. 2, p. 131. A former occupant, Robert Nicholas (d. 1667) was M.P. and Recorder of Devizes and one of the prosecuting counsel at the trial of Archbishop Laud in 1640.
49. Ex. info. Wiltshire Buildings Record.
50. *S.J.* 25 Aug. 1794.
51. *S.J.* vol. XLVI. 2249, 16 July 1781.
52. W.C. 2, p. 131.
53. W. Tunnicliffe, *A Topographical Survey of the Counties of Hants, Wilts, Dorset, Somerset, Devon and Cornwall* (1791).
54. Anstie, *General View*, p. 115.
55. Letter of Anstie to Lord Hawkesbury, 1808. P.R.O. H.O. 42/95.65.
56. Anstie, *Observations*, p. 12.
57. Anstie, *Letter to the Secretary of the Bath & West*, 1791, p. 10.
58. Anstie, *General View*, p. 59.
59. W.C. 6, p. 18. Advertisement of loss of snuffbox on the way to Calstone Mill.

60. M. Reeves and J. Morrison (eds.), *The Diaries of Jeffery Whitaker*, W.R.S., vol. 44 (Trowbridge, 1989).
61. Anstie, *Letter to the Secretary, Bath and West*, p. 18.
62. Anstie, *General View*, p. 46.
63. Anstie, *Observations*, p. 58.
64. Anstie, *General View*, pp. 95, 114.
65. Anstie, *An Answer*.

CHAPTER FOUR

Outrageous Fortune

A man that fortune's buffets and rewards
Hast ta'en with equal thanks.

Hamlet, III. i. 72.

The prosperous and dynamic pattern of Anstie's life was destined to be shattered by increasing stress, ill health, and ultimately business failure. Despite living to be eighty-seven, he was occasionally plagued by poor health, which on one occasion prevented him attending a wool meeting in London.[1] In 1786 he informed Mr Fawkener, Clerk to the Privy Council, that he could not attend a discussion on the French Treaty because he was 'indisposed this Morning with a complaint in his Bowells to whch he is much Subject when in London – and obliged to go a few miles into the Country'.[2] On another occasion he complained of being 'much disordered by the bile'.[3] Business and civic and public duties left him little chance of leisure. In 1791 he wrote:

> For a long time past I have enjoyed but little leisure to attend to anythng abstracted from my own business.[4]

While in Bath for his health, he was 'continually hindered by attention to other things of importance' and the 'necessity of often returning home in order to inspect my own business'.[5] He admitted that 'various matters were – unavoidably neglected while I was occupied in the Wool business'.[6]

Although Anstie described his situation in 1789 as 'affluent', with property worth £20,000,[7] he had borrowed heavily from his father, brother and sister to set up his business. His account book shows latent financial problems from 1788, when he

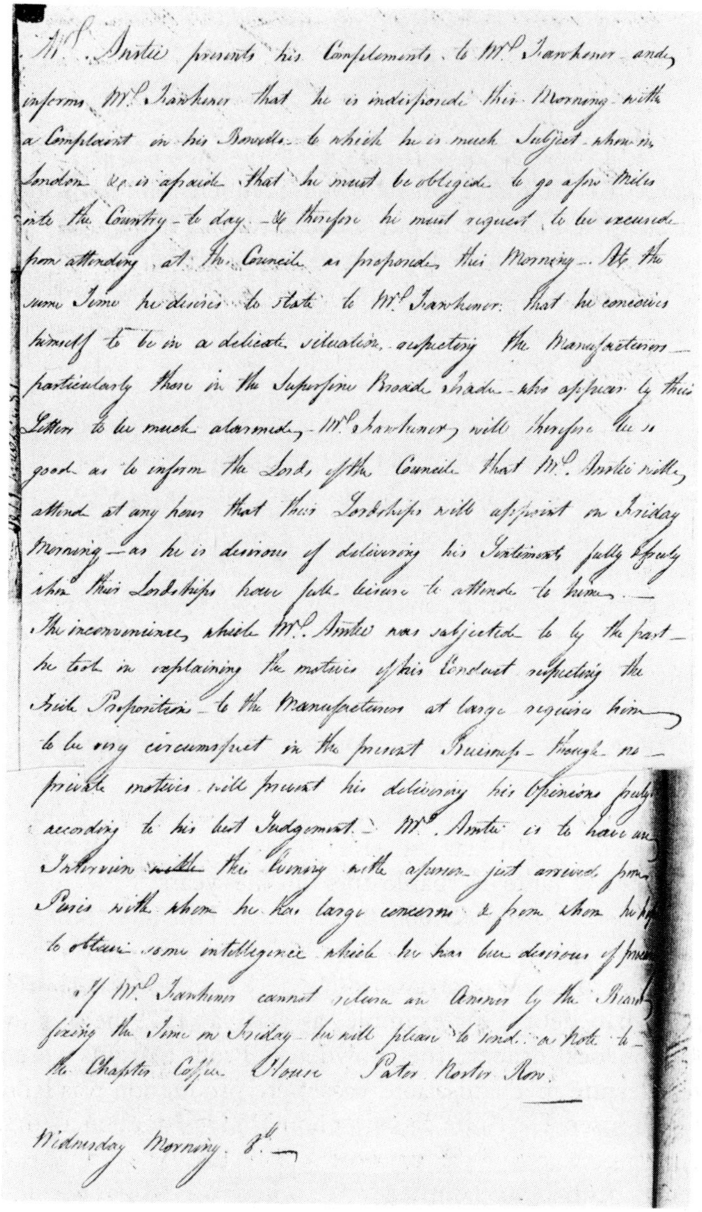

Mr. Anstie presents his Complements to Mr. Fawkener and informs Mr. Fawkener that he is indisposed this Morning with a Complaint in his Bowels to which he is much Subject when in London & is afraid that he must be obliged to go a few Miles into the Country to day — & therefore he must request to be excused from attending at the Council as proposed this Morning — At the same Time he desires to state to Mr. Fawkener that he conceives himself to be in a delicate situation respecting the Manufacturers — particularly those in the Superfine Broad Trade — who appear by their Letters to be much alarmed — Mr. Fawkener will therefore be so good as to inform the Lords of the Council that Mr. Anstie will attend at any hour that their Lordships will appoint on Friday Morning — as he is desirous of delivering his Sentiments fully & freely when their Lordships have full leisure to attend to him. — The inconvenience which Mr. Anstie was subjected to by the part he took in explaining the motives of his Conduct respecting the Irish Propositions to the Manufacturers at large requires him to be very circumspect in the present Business — though no private motives will prevent his delivering his Opinions fully according to his best Judgement. — Mr. Anstie is to have an Interview with this Evening with a person just arrived from Paris with whom he has large concerns & from whom he hopes to obtain some intelligence which he has been desirous of procuring. If Mr. Fawkener cannot return an Answer by the Bearer fixing the Time on Friday he will please to send a Note to the Chapter Coffee House Pater Noster Row.

Wednesday Morning 8th —

John Anstie's letter to Mr Fawkener in 1786

borrowed £2,186 18*s*. 4*d*. from his brother at 5% interest, which involved annual interest payments of £153. Benjamin, whose snuff business was prospering, also paid £856 5*s*. into Reed and Tylee's Bank in 1789 to settle some outstanding bills.[8] In 1788 Anstie borrowed £2,500 from the bank[9] and £200 from his mother.[10] By August 1790 he owed Stephen Hillman £500 for wool, but was only able to pay £125 a year in 1791 and 1792, the rest accruing interest.[11] There were evidently serious cash-flow problems. A page headed 'Law Charges, 1789–91' in Anstie's accounts lists journeys to Warminster and Marlborough Sessions, with expenses for 'Replivy and Indictment', perhaps indicating actions taken by him for the recovery of bad debts. These may be the 'important concerns requiring my immediate attention' to which he referred in his *Letter* of 1791. The general economic and political situation was also unfavourable. Increasing competition from Gloucestershire cassimere producers with the introduction of the gig mill, and the disturbed conditions in France, where he had a considerable trade, seriously affected his business. In 1793 some £17,500 worth of silk stocks and cloth on commission were stranded in Europe, and other debts due to him amounted to £40,363,[12] partly owing to the 'failure of a House in town'.[13] This may refer to a factor or a bank. None of the London banks listed in Anstie's accounts – Whitehead, Langston, Gosling or Staples – appears to have failed, but *The Salisbury Journal* lists several Blackwell Hall factors and London merchants as bankrupts in the years 1789 to 1791. Anstie himself owed £3,000 to Jeremiah Hill and Sons, merchants of Stephen Street, Bristol.[14] The scale of his operations meant that there was always likely to be a financial short fall through bad debts; for example, as early as 1779 he was owed £200 by a local draper, Joel Rowden.[15] Profit margins were not large. Despite mechanisation, cassimere production was labour- and skill-intensive. The factor Thomas Everitt calculated that labour constituted 35% of production costs,[16] and fine raw materials probably accounted for another 50%.[17] The rise in the price of Spanish wool, Anstie's concentration on the European

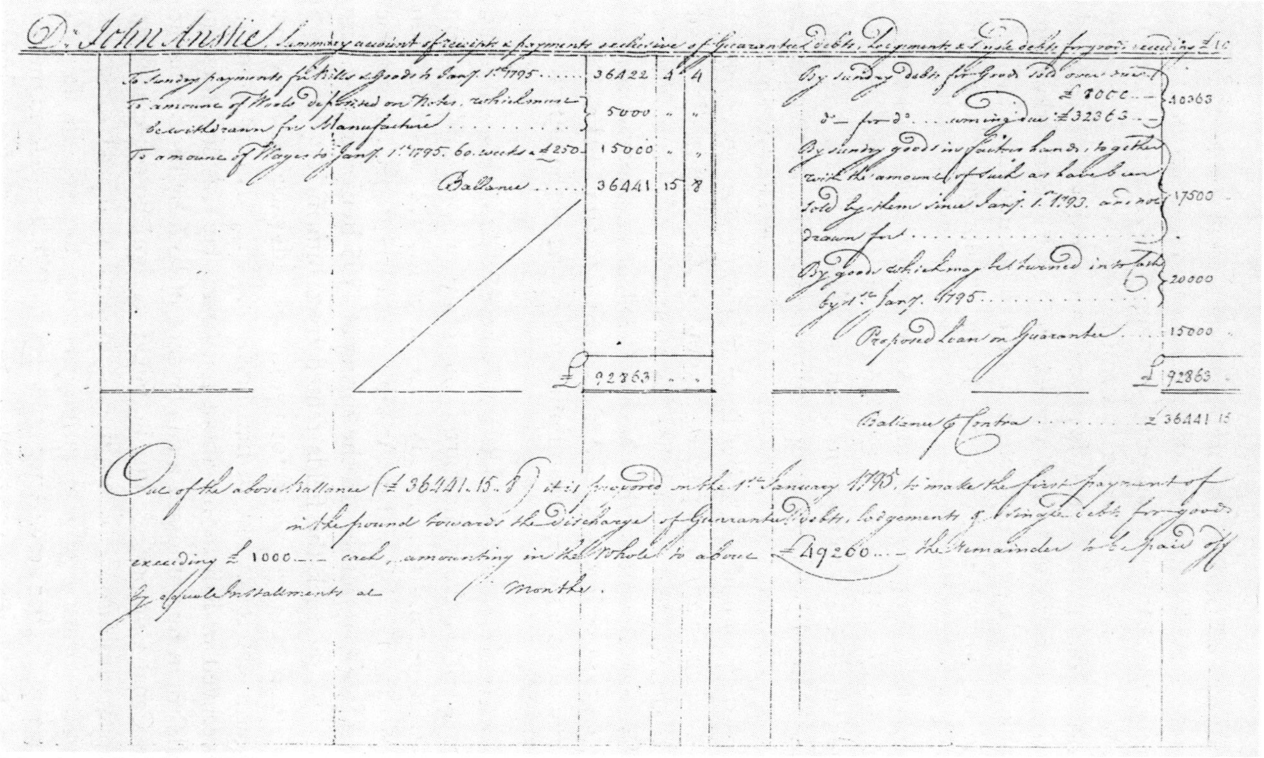

Dr. John Anstie. Summary account of receipts & payments exclusive of Guaranteed debts, Lodgements & single debts for goods exceeding £10

To Sundry payments for Bills & Goods to Jany. 1st 1795	36422	4	4	By sundry debts for Goods sold over due £8000 — d° — for d° … coming due £32363 —	40363
To amount of Wools deposited on Notes, which must be withdrawn for Manufacture	5000	"	"	By sundry goods in factors hands, together with the amount of such as have been sold by them since Jany. 1st 1793 and not drawn for	17500
To amount of Wages to Jany. 1st 1795. 60 weeks at £250	15000	"	"	By goods which may be turned into cash by 1st Jany. 1795	20000
Ballance	36441	15	8	Proposed Loan on Guarantee	15000
	£ 92863	"	"		£ 92863
				Ballance of Contra	£ 36441 15

Out of the above ballance (£ 36441.15.8) it is proposed on the 1st January 1795, to make the first payment of in the pound towards the Discharge of Guaranteed debts, lodgements & single debts for goods exceeding £ 1000 — each, amounting in the whole to above £49260 — the remainder to be paid off by equal Installments at Months.

John Anstie's debts, 1793

luxury market and the financial crisis of 1793 all played their part in his downfall. Perhaps from the start he was over-committed. He had ten establishments employed for various processes round Devizes, largely due to the lack of water in the town, which prevented him fully centralising and mechanising his operations in the same way as factory owners such as Richard Arkwright. Unlike such large manufacturers, he had not invested heavily in land and so had little diverse property to mortgage to stave off financial ruin.

Anstie's bankruptcy was announced in *The London Gazette* on 7 December 1793, and the Commission of Bankruptcy sat at *The Bear* on 20 and 21 of December and 18 January 1794.[18] To meet some of his debts it was proposed to sell £20,000 worth of goods and to take out a £15,000 loan. Anstie was anxious that his employees should not suffer from his financial collapse. Henry Collins, a servant, was paid eight months' salary up to 17 August 1794 and was lent £6 cash 'for his present need'.[19] In a letter of 1808 Anstie revealed that he had 'sunk a considerable sum of money by keeping employed from motives of humanity as well as public spirit a very great number of persons in the critical year 1792'.[20]

Anstie moved to live in Rowde, where he leased a small house (see overleaf), close and barn from John Love on £150 mortgate from Benjamin and £8 11*s*. annual rent. £12 was spent on improving the house but Anstie was clearly dependent on the charity of his brother. In the spring of 1795 Benjamin gave him £41 10*s*. to stock the fields rented from him in Rowde, which produced £19 a year, and four years later advanced £200 for 'his engagement to inform on making S. and P.'.[21] Anstie seems to have lived in Rowde for about ten years. He was still there in 1802 when he witnessed a conveyance of land by his brother to the Canal Company,[22] but he failed to sign the agreement for Baptist and Presbyterian inter-communion in 1807,[23] which suggests either a general withdrawal from local public life or a move to another area. After midsummer 1806 there is no further reference to him in the family account books, nor in the Rowde

John Anstie's house in Rowde

Land Tax, and an indenture of 1806, selling land in Rowde, gives his address as St. George's Fields, Surrey.[24] He does not appear in the Rowde Valuation of 1816.[25] It seems likely, therefore, that he moved to live with relatives in London. In 1808 he wrote to Lord Hawkesbury from Southwark, asking if there was any possibility of acquiring a situation. A friend had mentioned a forthcoming alteration in the management of the lottery business, involving additional commissioners; such a position would be 'very acceptable to John Anstie'. It was obviously galling to him to be 'wholly dependent on others for his support'.[26] In her will, his mother, who died in 1799, left £60 'for ye Board of my son John Anstie, his wife and child, Mariane' with £20 for mourning clothes.[27] Benjamin left him an annuity of £40 when he died in 1824.[28] These bequests and his own ultimate estate of £942 suggest considerably straitened circumstances.

Much of Anstie's land and property was sold or taken over by his brother, Benjamin, who converted Poulshot Mill for snuff grinding.[29] Anstie's Devizes factory was leased to the Overseers of the Poor for a House of Industry.[30] The family's woollen trade continued on a small retail scale for a little over ten years. An early nineteenth-century clothier's pattern book lists the Ansties' order for a sober, plain black cloth under 'Sundry Persons',[31] a sad contrast to the days when John Anstie's cloth was on sale in the capitals of Europe.

Anstie died in October 1830 in Wilson Street, Bristol, not far from his daughter's boarding school in Brunswick Square, and was buried in St. Paul's Churchyard, Portland Square, on 2 November 1830.[32] His obituary in the *Devizes Gazette* for 18 November paid tribute to his innovations in wool manufacture and his activities in the national economic sphere:

> To the energy and public spirit of this gentleman, the woollen manufacture of Wiltshire (and the West of England generally) was deeply indebted for its extension, and subsequent prosperity. His ingenuity and knowledge of the varieties of wool first suggested its combination with silk in the manufacture of fancy cloths, which he successfully introduced, and finally perfected to the

> exclusion of foreign competition. In the year 1788 [*sic*] he was appointed chairman of the Wool Committee for preparing evidence to be laid before Parliament respecting the importation of foreign wool, and ably furthered the object and interests of that Body, by enlarged views of a subject of national importance, at that period but imperfectly understood. His active benevolence is at this distant day remembered in the county of Wilts.

John Britton described him as 'a gentleman whose writings and exertions on behalf of English wools will ever reflect honour on his name'.[33]

Two of Anstie's favourite adjectives, 'liberal' and 'ingenuous', perhaps best sum up his character. Forward-looking and innovative, he supported new technological developments and economic policies, which were to be the basis of England's commercial and industrial ascendancy for a century. Yet he remained conscious of his social responsibilities, fulfilled through his concern for his own employees' welfare and his local philanthropic work. In many ways he typifies the late eighteenth-century cultured gentleman, with an important role in local affairs, an interest in new scientific and economic ideas and a sincere desire to promote 'the general good'.[34] On political issues he showed considerable independence of mind:

> No private means will prevent his delivering his opinions freely according to his best Judgement.[35]

He did not, however, indulge in negative political criticism:

> Influenced by no Party views, my principles will never lead me to obstruct the measures of Government merely for the sake of opposition.[36]

Nevertheless, he hoped 'never to be considered an enemy to freedom of enquiry on any subject',[37] and felt that 'an issue should be examined with care and attention, and judgement made from well-established facts and just reasoning', an attitude typical of eighteenth-century Rationalism. Superficially, Anstie's economic ideas seem ambivalent. He achieved tighter controls over the export of English wool, while at the same time advocating the freeing of international trade from protectionist tariffs. But Anstie was a pragmatist, and his overriding consideration was the national interest and 'the prosperity of the trade of the nation in general'. As both gentleman and manufacturer, he could approach the wool controversy free from prejudice and sectional interest, 'unbiassed and attentive to what shall appear of public benefit'.[38] Some of his views reflect the ideas of his contemporary, Jeremy Bentham (1742–1832) and his doctrine of 'the greatest happiness of the greatest number':

> Whatever circumstances the writer may be placed in, he trusts, in union with the most genuine and sincere desire to promote the welfare of the nation to which he belongs, he shall ever experience that spirit which impels the mind to seek for gratification in general happiness.

Anstie was fully aware of the blessings of peace, and trade's contribution to international understanding. The true interest of a nation, he felt, did not consist of 'continually exerting hostile acts against the trade and commerce of others'.

> How happy it would be for the world at large if, instead of the prevalent spirit of monopoly in trade, more generous and liberal views should prevail.[39]

Yet, paradoxically, throughout his life he was a staunch patriot and even considered military service, perhaps inspired by events in the Seven Years War. In 1779, at the height of the American War of Independence, France and Spain entered the war on the side of the colonists. Anstie described his reaction to this crisis:

> when the combined Fleets of France and Spain triumphed for a short time in the British Channel, he then armed and disciplined part of his Men, and, had an occasion offered, he would freely have led them to the hostile Field.[40]

This episode probably accounts for his possession in 1794 of 'thirty stand of muskets, with suitable military accoutrements'.[41] Anstie's deep patriotic feelings are revealed in this passage from one of his pamphlets:

> I can recollect no period of my life when the *Amor Patriae* did not glow in my breast, and though I was not destined to serve my country in the line which my early youth most approved, yet the same spirit which (had it not been checked by a mother's fears) would have led me to the possession of arms, has constantly actuated my conduct, and I am confident that my mind is superior to the contracted views of private interest, when that interest appears to be in opposition to the public good.[42]

Anstie's short but brilliant public career reflects some important trends in eighteenth-century life: the Enlightenment, the belief that conditions could be improved by thought and effort; the awakening interest in science and technology; the growing humanitarianism and philanthropy of the age; and the manufacturers' increasing influence and contribution in public life. In the eyes of Devizes historian James Waylen, Anstie 'exerted an influence of which he commanded an extensive share, in the advancement of objects of a patriotic kind' and was not only an eminent woollen manufacturer but 'a citizen in the best sense of the word'.[43] Anstie represents the caring eighteenth-century capitalist, with considerable leadership qualities, intellectual vigour and social conscience, for whom service to his country ran like a silk thread through the web of his life.

REFERENCES

1. Anstie, *General View*, p. 106.
2. Letter of Anstie to William Fawkener, 8 ? 1786. P.R.O., B.T. 6/111.
3. Letter of Anstie to Lord Hawkesbury, 26 June 1789, B.L. Add. Mss. 38224.172.
4. Anstie, *Letter*, 1791, p. 2.
5. Anstie, *General View*, p. 114.
6. Letter of Anstie to George Chalmers, n.d., B.L. Add. Mss. 38570.55.
7. Letter of Anstie to Lord Hawkesbury, 4 Feb. 1808. P.R.O., H.O. 42/95.
8. W.R.O. 212A/25. Anstie account books.
9. W.R.O. 212A/25.
10. Cons. Sarum. Reg. 11. fo. 185. Mary Anstie's will.
11. W.R.O. 1090/52. Stephen Hillman's ledgers.
12. W.R.O. 212A/25.
13. P.R.O., H.O. 42/95.65.

14. W.R.O. 212A/25.
15. W.R.O. 402/74. Joel Rowden's Bankruptcy Commission.
16. P.R.O., B.T. 6/113. Evidence of Thomas Everitt for the French Treaty.
17. Ponting, K., *The Special Characteristics of the West Country Woollen Industry* (1956), p. 11.
18. *S.J.* vol. LVIII, 9 December 1793.
19. W.R.O. 212A/25.
20. P.R.O., H.O. 42/95.65.
21. W.R.O. 212A/25.
22. G.W.R.A., Leases 3076, 3 November 1802.
23. W.R.O. 1270/28.
24. W.R.O. 212A/31/8. Rowde Land Deeds.
25. W.R.O. 1553/43. Rowde Valuation, 1816.
26. P.R.O., H.O. 42/95.65.
27. Cons. Sarum. Reg. 11. fo. 185. Mary Anstie's will 1799.
28. P.C.C. Reg. AB. no. 4. fo. 1529. Benjamin Anstie's will proved 6 Dec. 1824.
29. W.R.O. 529/230. Poulshot Mill leases.
30. W.R.O. H7/100/2, Box 1. Poor Law records.
31. W.R.O. 1553/55.
32. Bristol Record Office. St. Paul's Burial Records.
33. Britton, *Beauties*, vol. 2, p. 195.
34. Anstie, *General View*, p. 84.
35. P.R.O., B.T. 6/111. Evidence for Irish Treaty 1785.
36. *S.J.* vol. L. 2445, 18 April 1785.
37. Anstie, *Letter to Edward Phelips*, p. 26.
38. Anstie, *General View*, pp. 132–4.
39. Anstie, *Observations*, p. 94.
40. P.R.O., H.O. 42/95.65.
41. *S.J.* vol. LIX. 2933, 25 August 1794.
42. Anstie, *General View*, p. 105.
43. Waylen, J. *Chronicles of The Devizes* (1839), p. 352.

APPENDIX I

TEXTILE GLOSSARY

SOURCE: K. Ponting, *The Woollen Industry of South-West England* (Adams and Dart, Bath, 1971)

BEAVER	A heavy milled woollen cloth with a raised finish, resulting in a nap like a beaver's skin.
BILLY	Slubbings taken off the carding machine were joined and stretched and given a twist on the billy before being spun on the jenny.
BLACKWELL HALL	A London selling centre and wool supply depot for country traders, rebuilt in Basinghall Street after the Great Fire.
BROADCLOTH	Originally cloth made on a broad loom. Later a fine cloth woven in the plain weave but heavily fulled. West of England broadcloth was finer than Yorkshire cloth.
BURLING	Removal of vegetable matter and rectification of cloth faults in woollen fabrics.
CARDING	A preliminary treatment before spinning to open and mix the wool. Originally done by two hand-held cards covered with teasels, later with wire cards worked by horse driven machines. Narrow strips of wool were prepared with the fibres arranged lengthwise. Cards were made at Frome. The word derives from the Latin word for teasel, '*carduus*'.
CASSIMERE	A fine woollen cloth, from the French '*casimir*'.
COMBING	The preparatory process for long wools. The short fibre is removed and the top is spun into worsted yarn.

Raising the nap

FLEECE	Wool shorn from one sheep.
FLYING SHUTTLE	Kay's method 1733 of driving the shuttle across the loom mechanically, instead of moving it by hand.
FULLING or *TUCKING* or *MILLING*	The shrinking, thickening and firming of woollen cloth. Originally done by walking, later by water-wheel with Fuller's earth, obtainable to the south of Bath.
GIG	A teasel-covered machine for raising the nap on cloth.
JENNY	A multiple spinning-wheel using spindle or twist drafting,

Shearing

	invented by Hargreaves in 1764. First appeared in the West Country in 1775, and in Wiltshire in 1789.
NAP	Fibrous surface of cloth, raised to give a ribbed effect in the West Country.
OILING	To make the wool less brittle.
PIECE	A length of finished cloth, about 25 yards.
PRESSING	Finishing process, done between thick press papers.
RAISING	With teasels set in wooden cards to raise the nap.

RACK	A tenter frame with hooks for drying cloth.
SCOURING	The washing of raw or loose wool with stale urine and oil soap to remove the yolk or grease and perspiration.
SCRIBBLING	The first process of carding. The amount of wool needed was weighed and formed into a loose continuous fleece.
SERGE	A worsted warp.
SHEARING	Trimming the cloth surface.
SHUTTLE	The carrier of the weft across the loom.
SLUBBING	Piecing together, stretching and twisting the cardings on the billy ready for the jenny.
SPINDLE	Used to insert the twist into the yarn and to contain the spun yarn.
SPINNING	Manufacture of yarn.
WARP	Threads that run lengthwise.
WEAVING	Forming of fabric by crossing warp and weft.
WEFT	Threads that run across the cloth.
WILLEY	Used to open out the fibres and free them from impurities. Blends were selected to go forward for spinning.
WOOLLEN CLOTH	Wool woven from carded yarn in which the fibres are intermingled and lie in all directions, with a fluffy surface.
WORSTED	Cloth made from combed wool with the fibres lying parallel, with a smooth surface.

Appendix I

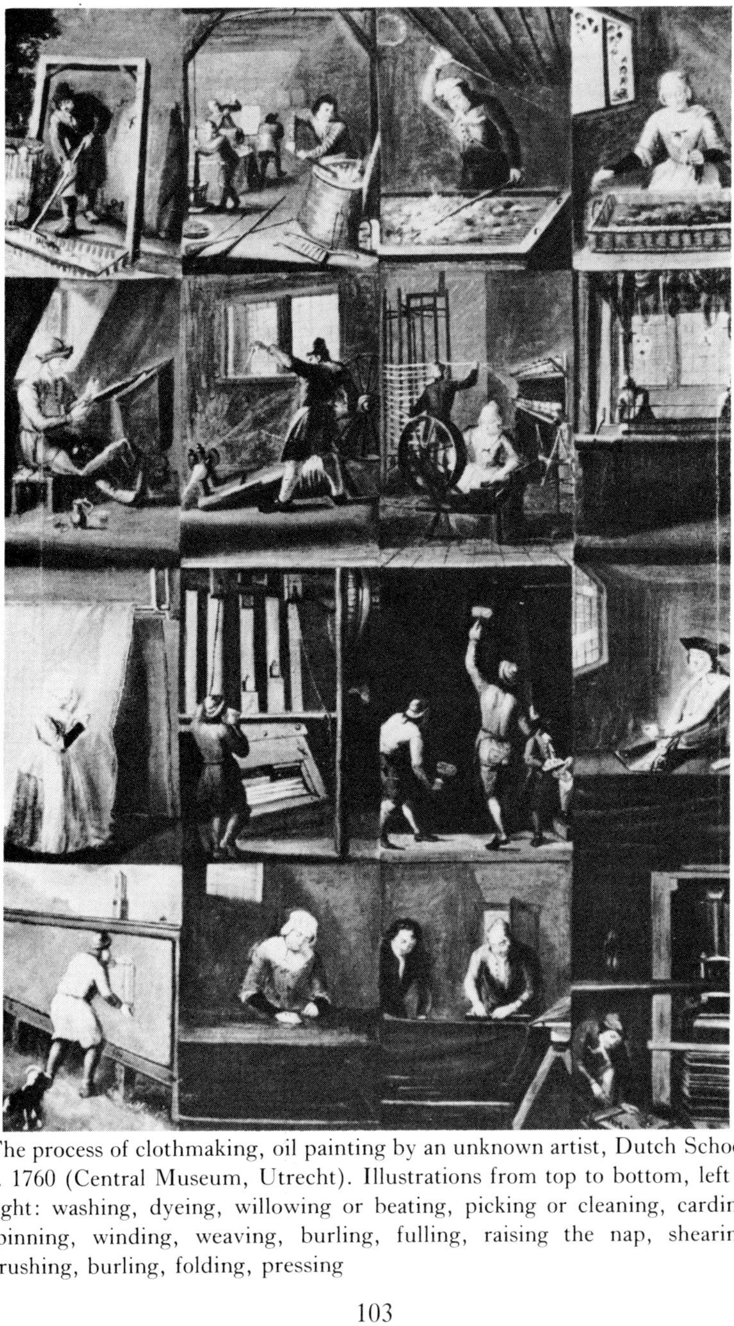

The process of clothmaking, oil painting by an unknown artist, Dutch School, *c.* 1760 (Central Museum, Utrecht). Illustrations from top to bottom, left to right: washing, dyeing, willowing or beating, picking or cleaning, carding, spinning, winding, weaving, burling, fulling, raising the nap, shearing, brushing, burling, folding, pressing

APPENDIX II

SUMMARY OF THE WOOL BILL

SOURCE: *The County Magazine*, August 1788

1788.

ABSTRACTS of ACTS paſſed in the laſt Seſſion of PARLIAMENT.

WOOL BILL.

EXPORTATION of SHEEP.

NO perſon ſhall bring, deliver, ſend, receive, or take, or cauſe or procure to be brought, delivered, ſent, received, or taken into any ſhip, veſſel, or boat, any live rams, ſheep, or lambs, of the breed of this kingdom, or the iſles of Jerſey, Guernſey, Sark, and Man, to be conveyed out of the ſaid kingdom, &c. into foreign parts, under forfeiture of the ſheep and veſſel to any perſons ſeizing the ſame; and the offenders, on conviction, with their aiders and abettors, to forfeit three pounds for every ſuch ſheep, &c. and to be committed to ſolitary confinement in the county gaol or houſe of correction for three calendar months, and until ſuch forfeiture be paid, not exceeding twelve calendar months; on a ſecond offence, the forfeiture to be five pounds and ſix months impriſonment, and in caſe of non-payment, not more than two years; ſuch forfeiture for the benefit of the perſons ſuing for the ſame. Wether ſheep, or wool growing on ſuch ſheep, carried alive in any veſſel for the neceſſary diet of the perſons therein, to be forfeited, unleſs licenſed by the comptroller or collector of the cuſtoms, or ſome other officer of his Majeſty's revenue.

EXPORTATION of the FLEECE, &c.

No perſon ſhall directly or indirectly export or otherwiſe convey, or cauſe to be conveyed out of this kingdom, &c. any wool whatſoever of the growth of this kingdom, &c. or any woolfels, mortlings, ſhortlings, yarn or worſted made of wool, woolflocks, crewels, coverlids, waddings, or other manufactures, or pretended manufactures, made of wool ſlightly wrought up, or otherwiſe put together, ſo as the ſame may be reduced and made uſe of as wool again, or mattreſſes or beds ſtuffed with combed wool, or wool fit for combing or carding, or any fullers earth, &c. under forfeiture, for the firſt offence, of three ſhillings for every pound weight of ſuch wool, &c. or the ſum of fifty pounds in the whole, at the election of the perſon or perſons who ſhall ſue for the ſame, and ſolitary impriſonment for the ſpace of three calendar months, and until the penalty ſhall be paid; the whole of ſuch impriſonment not to exceed the ſpace of twelve calendar months; on the ſecond offence, the penalty to be the ſame, and the impriſonment ſix months and until the penalty ſhall be paid, the whole of ſuch impriſonment not to exceed the ſpace of two years; all which forfeitures ſhall be for the benefit of the perſons who ſhall ſue for the ſame; and the ſaid wool, &c. together with the veſſel, carriage, horſes, or other beaſts, on or by which any of the ſaid prohibited articles ſhall be loaded or conveying, ſhall be liable to be ſeized, and ſhall become forfeited for the benefit of the perſon or perſons who ſhall ſeize the ſame.

ENTRY of WOOL.

A due entry to be made of the ſaid wool, &c. at the port from which the ſame ſhall be intended to be conveyed, containing the exact weight, marks, and numbers of the ſame, before lading or carrying away any of the ſaid wool, &c. within five miles of any ſuch port or place on the ſaid ſea coaſts, from which the ſame is or are to be conveyed; and if any wool, &c. ſhall be carrying towards the ſea for the purpoſe aforeſaid, without being entered as aforeſaid, and without being accompanied with a certificate of ſuch entry, the wool, &c. ſo found, and alſo the horſes, carriages, &c. ſhall be forfeited for the benefit of the perſon or perſons who ſhall ſeize thereupon.

REMOVAL of WOOL.

Wool may be carried from the place of ſhearing to the dwelling-houſes or outhouſes thereunto belonging, though the ſame be within five miles or leſs of the ſea, if within ten days after the ſhearing of the ſaid wool, and before the removal or otherwiſe diſpoſal of the ſame, or any part thereof, from the place where it was carried after ſhearing. Certificates to be made to the officers of the cuſtoms in the next adjacent port, of the number of fleeces, and where the ſame is houſed, and three days at leaſt before ſuch removal; on failure thereof be liable to the penalties expreſſed in the foregoing clauſe. If ſuch next adjacent port ſhould happen to be at a greater diſtance than five miles from the dwelling-houſe or houſes of ſuch aforeſaid perſons, then notice or certificate ſhall be given to the neareſt juſtice of the peace, or officer of his Majeſty's revenue.

WOOL not to be removed betwixt Sun ſetting and riſing.

No wool, or any other of the aforeſaid woollen or worſted articles, ſhall be removed or carried towards the ſea, within five miles of the ſea-coaſt, upon any pretence whatever, between ſun ſetting and ſun riſing, upon pain of the ſame being forfeited, with the horſes, carriages, &c. for the benefit of the perſon or perſons ſeizing the ſame; and the driver or drivers of ſuch carriage knowing thereof ſhall, on conviction, be committed to the houſe of

Appendix II

THE COUNTY MAGAZINE

correction for one month. The grower of wool may remove at any time, after sun setting, such wool as shall have been shorn that day, from the place of shearing to the store-house of such wool grower, although within five miles of the sea-coast.

To prevent Evasion of the Act.

No person except an officer of his Majesty's customs, excise or salt duties, who shall have cause to suspect that any sheep, wool, or any of the before enumerated articles, and which are hereby prohibited from being exported, is or are conveying, contrary to the true meaning of this act, may examine or seize such sheep, wool, &c. other than together and in company with a constable, or other officer of the peace, or any officer of his Majesty's customs, excise or salt duties, who are hereby required, on application being made to him or them, immediately to attend the person or persons applying for such assistance; on failure whereof, every such constable, &c. shall forfeit and pay for every such offence the sum of twenty pounds.

Punishment for obstructing the Execution of the Act.

Any person who shall obstruct or molest another in the making or attempting to make such seizures as aforesaid, and shall be convicted of the said offences, shall, by order of the court before whom such offender or offenders shall be convicted, be transported to some place beyond the seas for a term not exceeding seven years.

Punishment for false winding.

It is enacted, that all persons who shall wind, or cause to be wound, any fleeces of wool not being sufficiently washed, or wind or cause to be wound within any fleece, clay, lead, stones, sand, tails, deceitful locks, cots, cals, comber, lamb's wool, or any other thing whereby the fleece might be made more weighty, to the deceit and loss of the buyer, shall forfeit for every such fleece two shillings, the whole whereof shall be paid to the finder or prover of the above-mentioned deceits; and the offences against the said act from henceforth shall and may be proceeded upon, heard, and determined, by and before any one justice of the peace residing at or near the place where such offence or offences shall be committed, in a summary way. The seller of wool, touching which any complaint or information shall have been made, may apply to the justice of the peace before whom the information shall have been laid, who may hear and determine the matter of complaint; and if it shall then appear, to the satisfaction of the said justice, that the wool then complained of had been actually wound or folded falsely and deceitfully by the person then charged by the seller thereof with having wound and folded the same, and that without the privity, knowledge, or consent of such seller, that then, and in every such case, the person who had actually wound or folded such wool shall be subject to the penalties herein before imposed upon the seller.

Appeal to the Quarter Sessions.

Any person thinking himself aggrieved by the judgment or determination of any such justice of the peace, may appeal to the next general or quarter sessions of the peace to be held for the county, division, or place, in and for which such justice shall have acted.

Winder's Oath to be administered at the Quarter Sessions.

The justices of the peace who shall hereafter be assembled at any general quarter sessions of the peace, or any adjournment thereof, are empowered to administer the oath to every such person as shall be desirous of becoming a sworn winder of wool, and shall produce a certificate under the hands of any two growers of wool, testifying, to the satisfaction of such justices, that such person is properly qualified to become a sworn winder of wool. Provided always, and be it enacted, that nothing herein contained shall be construed to hinder or prevent any one from employing any person in the winding or folding of wool, although such person shall not have been sworn in manner before-mentioned.

Outside Passengers on Stage-Coaches, &c.

ALL carriages travelling for hire are included in this bill. From and after the first of November, 1788, no carriage of the above description is to suffer more than six persons as outside passengers, that is, two beside the driver upon the box, and four upon the roof; every driver taking more, shall for every person over forfeit forty shillings. If the driver should happen to be the owner, he must pay four pounds. Either master or man to be committed for non-payment to the prison or house of correction nearest where the offence is committed, without bail, for not less than one month, unless the penalty is sooner paid.

If an offender refuse to tell his name before a justice, he shall be committed.

Constables refusing to execute warrants issued under this act, shall pay forty shil-

APPENDIX III

BIOGRAPHICAL SUMMARIES

Set out below are details of Anstie's contemporaries and associates mentioned in the text.

SOURCES: *Dictionary of National Biography*, Wiltshire Cuttings Collection in W.A.S. Library

HENRY ADDINGTON (1757–1844)

Lawyer, politician and friend of Pitt. Recorder of Devizes 1784–1828. M.P. for Devizes 1784–1805. In 1791 gave the town £500 to rebuild The Shambles and in 1814 donated the Market Cross. Speaker of the House of Commons 1789–1801. Prime Minister 1801–4. Home Secretary 1812–22, when he was associated with a repressive policy.

DR JAMES ANDERSON (1739–1808)

Scottish economist, agricultural writer and pamphleteer. In 1790 he started an Edinburgh paper *The Bee* on economic topics.

RICHARD ARKWRIGHT (1732–92)

Cotton manufacturer and landowner. Invented water frame for spinning in 1769 and crank and comb for carding in 1775. Built mill and industrial village at Cromford, Derbyshire 1784. Introduced day and night shift work, but was an enlightened employer, providing societies, markets and entertainment for his workers. Knighted in 1786.

SIR JOSEPH BANKS (1743–1820)

Explorer, botanist and patron of science. Accompanied Cook's expedition 1768–71. Became Fellow of the Royal Society in 1766 and its President in 1778. Wrote an anonymous pamphlet, *The Propriety of Allowing a Qualified Exportation of Wool* (1782). Left his collections to the British Museum.

Appendix III

JEREMY BENTHAM (1748–1832)

Friend of Lord Shelburne. Lawyer and writer on jurisprudence and political economy. Exponent of the political principles of utilitarianism and 'the greatest happiness of the greatest number'.

MATTHEW BOULTON (1728–1809)

Engineer, son of a Birmingham silver stamper. Established a factory at Soho, 1772. Partnered James Watt in the production of steam engines. Fellow of the Royal Society and member of the Lunar Society.

GEORGE CHALMERS (1742–1825)

Scottish antiquarian, historian and biographer. Chief Clerk to the Board of Trade from 1787.

THOMAS COKE (1752–1842)

Descendant of Lord Chief Justice in James I's reign. Landowner and agricultural improver. Transformed his estate at Holkham, Norfolk, into a centre of agricultural life, with annual sheep-shearing and ploughing matches. M.P. for Norfolk 1776–1832. Zealous Whig and Fox supporter and friend of the Prince of Wales, later George IV. He was created Earl of Leicester in 1837.

SIR JOHN DALRYMPLE (1726–1810)

Scottish lawyer, author and pamphleteer. Baron of the Exchequer 1776–1807.

JOHN DUNNING (1731–83)

Lawyer. Through the influence of Lord Shelburne, became M.P. for Calne 1768. Supported Shelburne's opposition to the Government's American policy and his bill to remove Roman Catholics' disabilities. Became Baron Ashburton and Chancellor of the Duchy of Lancaster in Shelburne's Ministry 1782–3.

WILLIAM EDEN (1744–1814)

Statesman, diplomat and M.P. On Committee of Trade and Plantations 1785, he negotiated the Commercial Treaty with France 1785–6. Ambassador to Spain 1788 and Holland 1789. Became Baron Auckland 1789 and President of Board of Trade 1806–7.

CHARLES JAMES FOX (1749–1806)

Whig M.P. and orator. Political opponent of Pitt and critic of George III's Ministers, their American policy and corruption. Championed French Revolution.

CHARLES JENKINSON (1729–1809)

M.P. and Privy Councillor. Held Government office at Trade, Treasury and War under Grenville, Grafton, North and Pitt. Leader of The King's Friends after Bute's retirement and had great influence at Court. Became Lord Hawkesbury 1786 and Earl of Liverpool 1796.

LORD SHELBURNE, 1st MARQUESS OF LANSDOWNE (1737–1805)

Landowner and Chathamite politician. Supported Parliamentary reform, Catholic Emancipation, Free Trade and conciliation towards America. Held several Government offices. Prime Minister 1782–3. Patron of science, literature and the arts. His houses, Bowood in Wiltshire and Lansdowne House in London, became centres of literary and liberal society.

GEORGE SLOPER (1710–1821)

Devizes master baker. Mayor 1781, 1791 and 1800, and holder of many other local offices. Kept a diary of local and international events 1753–1810.

JOSIAH WEDGWOOD (1730–95)

Staffordshire master potter. Introduced division of labour into his factories and improved ceramic design. Became Queen's Potter 1762 and established works at Etruria 1769. In 1783 became a Fellow of the Royal Society.

FRANCIS YERBURY (1707–78)

Came from Royalist landowning family. Career as lawyer near Spitalfields. Suggested the introduction of some of the techniques used in the silk industry to the wool trade. Patent for cassimeres 1766.

ARTHUR YOUNG (1741–1820)

Agricultural writer and publicist of enclosures and new farming methods. Wrote description of his tours through England, France and Ireland, and produced many of the *General Views*. Until 1809 edited the monthly *Annals of Agriculture*, to which George III and Jeremy Bentham contributed. Secretary to the Board of Agriculture 1793. Founded The Farmers Club.

SELECT BIBLIOGRAPHY

MANUSCRIPT SOURCES

Bath Record Office:

Bath and West Society Papers, 1777–1811

British Library:

Add. Mss 22903, 38224, 38390, 38570. Anstie's Letters

British Museum:

B.M. (SC) I–IV. The Banks Sheep and Wool Papers

Guildhall Library, London

Ms. 11, 936. Anstie's Sun Fire Insurance Policies

Public Record Office, Kew:

B.T. 5–6. Board of Trade records. Evidence on the French and Irish trade treaties

H.O. 42/95. Letter from Anstie to Lord Hawkesbury, 1808

Details of the extensive manuscript sources used in W.A.S. Library in Devizes and in the Wiltshire Record Office in Trowbridge can be obtained from the notes deposited by the author at W.A.S. Library, 41 Long Street, Devizes.

PRINTED SOURCES

(Place of publication is London, unless otherwise stated)

I. PRIMARY

i. Directories

Bailey's Western and Midland Directory, or The Merchant's and Tradesman's Useful Companion (Pearson & Rollason, 1783)

The Universal Directory of Trade, Commerce and Manufacture, 5 vols., vol. 2., *Wiltshire* (Barfoot, P., and Wilkes, J., 1791).

ii. Magazines

The County Magazine for the Years 1786 & 1787, particularly dedicated to the Inhabitants of Berkshire, Dorsetshire, Hampshire, Somersetshire and Wiltshire (Collins, Salisbury, 1788)

The Gentleman's Magazine, vols. 56 (1786) and 61 (1791)

iii. Maps

W.A.S. Library:

Andrews, J., and Dury, A., *Topographical Map of the County of Wiltshire* (1773)

Dore, Edward, *Plan of the Ancient Borough of Devizes* (1759)

W.R.O.:

Overton, John, *Map of the South Ward of Devizes* (1737–8), W.R.O. 1553/87

iv. Newspapers

Bath Chronicle, Bath Herald, Devizes & Wiltshire Gazette, Salisbury & Winchester Journal, Simpson's Salisbury Gazette

v. Pamphlets

Bath University Library, Special Collections:

Anstie, John, *An Answer to Those who have read Sir John Dalrymple's Pamphlet in support of a Tax and Permission to export raw wool* (1782)

Bodleian Library, Oxford:

Anstie, John, A General View of the Bill presented to Parliament during the last Session for preventing the illicit Exportation of British Wool and Live Sheep (1787). Bod. G. Pamph. 1190/7

British Library:

Anstie, John, *A Letter addressed to Edward Phelips Esq. on the Advantages of manufacturing the combing wool of England which is smuggled to France* (1788). B.L.102.h.52.

——, *Observations on the Importance and Necessity of Introducing Improved Machinery into the Woollen Manufactory* (1803). B.L. 1138.i.2.(2)

Banks, Sir Joseph, *The Propriety of Allowing a qualified Exportation of Wool discussed historically* (1782)

vi. Record Society Publications

Beckinsale, R. (ed.), *The Trowbridge Woollen Industry*, W.R.S. 6 (Devizes, 1951)

Dale, C. (ed.), *Wiltshire Apprentices and their Masters*, W.R.S. 17 (Devizes, 1961)

vii. State Papers

House of Lords Main Papers: Evidence for Wool Bill 1788

Journal of The House of Commons, vols. 41, 43.

ix. Miscellaneous

Cunnington, B. (ed.), *Some Annals of the Borough of Devizes, 1553–1791* (Simpson, Devizes, 1925)

Letters and Papers on Agriculture, Planting etc, addressed to the Society instituted at Bath for the Encouragement of Agriculture, Arts, Manufacture and Commerce within the Counties of Somerset, Wiltshire, Gloucestershire and Dorset and the City and County of Bristol, vols. 1–14 (Cruttwell, Bath 1792–1807)

Smith, J., *Chronicon Rusticum Commerciale or Memoirs of Wool* (1747)

Tunnicliffe, W., *A Topographical Survey of the Counties of Hants, Wilts, Dorset, Somerset, Devon and Cornwall* (B.C. Collins, Salisbury, 1791)

Young, A., *The Annals of Agriculture* (1784–1815)

Select Bibliography

II. SECONDARY

i. Books

Aubrey, J., *Wiltshire*; *Topographical Collections*, (ed. J.E. Jackson) (Henry Bull, Devizes, 1862)

Bradby, E., *The Book of Devizes* (Buckingham, 1985)

Britton, J., *The Beauties of Wiltshire Displayed in Statistical, Historical and Descriptive Sketches, interspersed with Anecdotes of the Arts* (2 vols., J.D. Dewick, 1801), vol. 2

Coleman, D.C., *Sir Joseph Banks, Baronet and Businessman* (Clarendon Press, Oxford, 1963)

Crittall, E., (ed.), *The Victoria History of the County of Wiltshire* vol. 8 (1965) and vol. 10 (1975)

Davis, T., *A General View of the Agriculture of the County of Wiltshire* (W. Smith, 1794)

Department of the Environment, *List of Buildings of Special Architectural or Historic Interest*, Borough of Devizes (D.o.E., 1972)

Harte, N.B. and Ponting, K.G., *Textile History & Economic History – Essays in Honour of Miss Julia de Mann* (Manchester U.P., 1973)

Lillywhite, B., *London Coffee Houses* (Allen, & Unwin, 1963)

Mann, J. de L., *The Cloth Industry in the West of England from 1640 to 1880* (O.U.P., 1971)

——, *Clothiers and Weavers during the Eighteenth Century* – reprinted from *Studies in the Industrial Revolution, Essays Presented to T.S. Ashton* (1960)

O'Brien, P., *Joseph Banks, A Life* (Collins Harvill, 1987)

Ponting, K., *The Special Characteristics of the West Country Woollen Industry* (International Wool Secretariat, 1956)

——, *The West of England Cloth Industry* (Macdonald, 1957)

——, *The Woollen Industry of South-West England* (Adams & Dart, Bath, 1971)

Pugh, R., (ed) *The Victoria History of the County of Wiltshire*, vol. 4 (1959)

Ramsay, G., *The Wiltshire Woollen Industry in the Sixteenth and Seventeenth Centuries* (Frank Cass & Co., 1943)

Rogers, K., *Warp and Weft: The Somersetshire and Woollen Industry* (Buckingham, 1986)

——, *Wiltshire and Somerset Woollen Mills* (Pasold Research Fund, Edington, 1976)

Warner, Rev. R., *The Modern History of Bath* (Bath, 1801)

Waylen, J., *Chronicles of the Devizes* (Longman, 1839)

——, *A History Military and Municipal of the Ancient Borough of Devizes* (Devizes, 1859)

ii. Journal Articles

Brown, W.E., 'Long's Stores', *W.A.M.* vol. 55 (1953), pp. 139–45

Morris, J., 'The West of England Woollen Industry 1750–1840', *Bulletin of the Institute of Historical Research*, vol. 13 (1935), pp. 106–10

Ponting, K., 'Wiltshire Woollen Mills; Insurance Returns 1753–1771', *W.A.M.* vol. 69 (1974), pp. 161–72.

Willoughby, R., 'Water Mills in West Wiltshire', *W.A.M.* vol. 64 (1969) pp. 71–99

iii. Miscellaneous

W.A.S. Cuttings, Prints and Tracts Collections

INDEX